Overcoming Challenges to Loving Your Wife

Living the Love of Christ
Dr. Darrell D. Rose

Counseling and the Cross Publishers

To my wife wonderful wife Cynthia, for your exceptional support in making me the Godly man that I am today

To my Sons, Aaron and Jonathan, to help you become the best Christ-Like husband that God would have you to be.

Contents

Introduction

Welcome to "Overcoming the Challenges of Loving Your Wife: Living the Love of Christ."

Marriage can be one of life's greatest joys, but it can also be one of its greatest challenges. Many husbands struggle to love their wives well. For some, the challenge comes from feeling disrespected, unheard, or opposed. Others think their wives view them as incompetent, talk down to them, or refuse to submit to their leadership. Still others struggle because they don't know what biblical love looks like in practice.

Moreover, most men equate love with provision — working hard, protecting their families, and providing the necessities of life. While these are important, they fall short of the love Christ commands. Scripture calls husbands to *"love your wives, just as Christ also loved the church and gave Himself up for her"* (Ephesians 5:25). But what does that mean in daily life? Some Christian men are familiar with this command but lack a clear understanding of how to live it out in practice. Others understand it but are stuck in bitterness, unforgiveness, or frustration.

The truth is, loving your wife as Christ loves the church is a **God-sized task** — and no man can do it in his own strength. Too often, we try with willpower, determination, or sheer grit, but without Christ and the power of the Holy Spirit, we fall short.

So where do you turn when love feels impossible? How can you overcome the challenges of loving your wife? What hope, if any, exists when a marriage is cold, distant, or hostile? How do you love your wife when she seems to reject or disrespect you? These are the questions that inspired this book.

Why This Book Matters

This book will not simply give you quick tips or surface-level advice. Instead, it will guide you through the life of Christ, illustrating how His example teaches us to love in the most challenging situations. Jesus faced some of the same challenges that we face as we seek to love our wives. This book aims to show you how to overcome the difficulties of loving your wife by living the love of Christ. As you journey through the pages of this book, you will learn how to:

- Define love biblically, not culturally.

- Recognize roadblocks that keep you from loving well.

- Examine how Christ responded to opposition and rejection

- Apply Christlike love to real marital struggles.

- Reflect God's character — His mercy, patience, grace, and forgiveness — in your marriage in the face of adversity.

Loving your wife isn't about convenience or comfort. It's about glorifying God. And when you love her with Christ's love, the blessings ripple outward — into your home, your children, your church, and even future generations.

A Call to Husbands

You may feel like your marriage is too far gone. And if there is hope in repairing and restoring your marriage, where do you begin? Or perhaps you've thought, *"We've been in trouble too long. Maybe it's beyond repair."* But God's Word says otherwise. With Him, nothing is impossible. Transformation begins when you humble yourself before the Lord, seek His wisdom, and allow His Spirit to change your heart.

The starting point is not fixing your wife, but letting God refine *you*. Ask Him for eyes to see yourself as He sees you. True victory begins with self-awareness, shaped by His Word.

Ultimately, loving your wife flows from your reverence for God. Your purpose is to glorify Him by conforming to the image of His Son, even when that means suffering and sacrifice. Christ's love was not dependent on being loved in return, and neither should yours be. When you love your wife unconditionally, God promises blessings and rewards:

"Give, and it will be given to you. They will pour into your lap a good measure—pressed down, shaken together, and running over. For by your standard of measure it will be measured to you in return." (Luke 6:38 NASB)

Psalm 128:1-4 (NLT) says,

"How joyful are those who fear the LORD— all who follow His ways! You will enjoy the fruit of your labor. How joyful and prosperous you will be! Your wife will be like a fruitful vine flourishing within your home. Your children will be like vigorous young olive trees as they sit around your table. That is the LORD's blessing for those who fear Him."

As you start this journey, pray with me:

"Lord, help me to love my wife as Christ loved the church and gave Himself up for her. Teach me to live with her in an understanding way, showing her honor as a fellow heir of the grace of life, so that my prayers will not be hindered." (1 Peter 3:7 NASB)

Chapter 1
Where is the Love?

"I Want a Divorce"

After arriving home from work one night, my wife served me dinner as usual. However, I know that tonight will be different. I have mustered enough courage to ask for a divorce. I raised the topic as calmly as I could. She didn't seem angry at first, but she asked me softly, "Why?"

I could not answer, so I avoided giving a detailed explanation. This upset her. That night we slept without talking to each other. I could hear her sobbing the whole night. I know that it is really hard for her not to know what went wrong with our relationship. But how can I tell her that I am seeing someone else?

The next morning, I drafted a divorce settlement and presented it to her. However, she tore it into pieces in front of me and went away. I felt a sense of guilt, and I knew it wasn't her fault that we drifted away from each other, but it had already happened. I fell out of love with her. Besides, I already have plans with the new love of my life.

The following day, I came home very late and found her writing something. I went straight to bed without talking to her. The next morning, she told me about her divorce conditions. One of which shocked me. She requested that I carry her out of our bedroom every morning. I thought this was a usurp request, but I agreed nonetheless to get this over with.

We didn't have any body contact for as long as I can remember, so the first day seemed awkward. Our son cheered on us, not knowing that this was more of a farewell gesture than an expression of love. For the next 30 days, we did the same routine, and gradually, I felt some of the loss of intimacy returning. I also noticed that she had matured {aged} and lost a lot of weight, probably because of the stress of our impending divorce. At the end of 30 days, our son came into our room and reminded me it was about time for his mom. This has been a daily routine that my son has come to expect every morning. My wife embraced him dearly. I turned away because I thought I might have a change of heart at the last minute. She wrapped her hand around my neck as I held her in my arms, walking from our room to the dining area. I had her so close that she could almost hear her heartbeat, exactly like the day of our honeymoon. I finally admitted to myself that our relationship lacked intimacy and not love. I went straight to the other woman and called off our relationship.

"I have to make things right," I told myself as I bought some flowers for my dear wife. I must apologize and tell her how much I still love her.

With flowers in my hands, a smiling face, with excitement, I ran into our room to find my wife in bed...dead. She kept it a secret that she had been battling cancer and only had a month to live. She wanted to make it seem that I was a good husband in front of our son's eyes. Up to her last moment, this woman only made me look better to others than I really was.[1] (Story by Guy Njoukam)

Where is the Love?

Do you still love your spouse as much as on your wedding day? Has your love grown deeper, or has it withered under the pressures of daily life?

Think back to dating: the excitement, the long conversations, the intentional gestures. We did everything possible to win our wives' hearts. But somewhere after "I do," for many husbands, that passion fades. Instead of romance, there are arguments. Instead of gentleness, there is criticism. Instead of intimacy, there is distance.

You may not have spoken the words "I want a divorce," but perhaps the thought crossed your mind.

Most husbands know all too well the excitement we experienced when we dated our wives. We always put our best foot forward. We had our pre-date routine. Before going on a date, we took refreshing showers, put on nice clothing, splashed on our best cologne, ensured we had a fresh haircut, cleaned our cars, and then zoomed out into the night to meet, greet, and romance the remarkable woman in our lives. Wherever she wanted to go was OK with you. Whatever restaurant she chose for dinner was no problem. Whatever movie she wanted to see was completely OK with us. We would do anything she wanted to impress her and win her favor. Some of us offered foot massages, warm touches, and gentle kisses or chose to express our love with flowers, chocolates, and love letters. You both just seemed to connect. Whenever there was a disagreement or an argument, one of you took the initiative to call the other person and say, "I'm sorry," to restore the relationship because you realized that your love for one another was much more valuable than the issue at hand. And as far as communication goes, you would spend hours upon hours talking with her on the phone at night and send countless text messages during the day. Then one day, you realize that you are in love with her. She has become the woman of your life! So, you work up enough nerve to propose marriage to her while worrying about her answer.

After she said, "Yes," you are off to the wedding day with all the bells and whistles. Your families and friends are witnesses to the exchange of vows between the two of you in the presence of God-Ordained authority, typically an officiating minister. Immediately after you kiss your Bride, you and your new wife receive special honors from all of your wedding guests. Everyone enjoys the festivities, including borage of hors d'oeuvres, music, dancing, dinner, sparkling champagne, chocolate-covered strawberries, and wedding cake. You enjoyed your honeymoon together, and the first few months to a year seem great.

Then things slowly began to change. It appears the woman you married is not the same woman you fell in love with. There is so much about her that you did not know. You realize that there is a significant gap between you and her. If what you knew then, before saying, "I Do," is what you know now, you probably would have reconsidered. She used to be a giving person; now, she appears selfish. She wants everything her way. She respected you when dating, but now she is very disrespectful. She is easily angered and tends to blow up about every little thing. She is full of drama; every day, there is a new episode of grumbling and complaining. You come home after a long day at work to a home that should be a place of peace, but your home, your place of refuge and peace, has become a place of turmoil, agitation, and distress. You used to be able to talk to her about anything. Now, you avoid conversation with her because every attempt to communicate with her seems to end in an argument. When a dispute occurs, she blows up, storms off into the bedroom, slams the door, and you shut down or leave the house for a while, hoping that things will settle down.

Where is the love? Better yet, how can you love someone who seems so hard to love? You are so opposite from one another and argue about petty stuff. When you say "up," she says "down." When you say "right," she says "left." She says it is just right when you say it is too hot. You say, *"I want the window down,"* and she says, "No, *I want it up.*" Intimacy is no longer there. You no longer even kiss and touch one another as much as you used to. You feel unappreciated, and nothing is ever good enough. She seems to find fault in everything you do.

Now you've reached a point where you are considering throwing in the towel. Unlike the end of the story at the beginning of this chapter, your spouse has not physically died, but it feels like your marriage is dead. You have tried to talk with her and share your heart, but your spouse seems to add meaning to what you have said, and now you find yourself arguing about something you did not say. Finally, like the husband in the story, someone, either you or your wife, mustered up enough courage to say those dreadful words, "I want a divorce" or "Maybe we need a break from each other." You may not have said those words, but the thought of parting ways may have crossed your mind.

The Tragedy of Divorce

Marriages across our nation are crumbling. Divorce rips apart not just homes, but hearts. It leaves men and women emotionally, mentally, and spiritually broken.

Some stories end in shocking rage, like the man who literally cut his house in half with a chainsaw during divorce proceedings. Others end in devastating violence, like the tragic shooting of a woman by her estranged husband in Oakland. Not every divorce ends so dramatically, but each one leaves scars.

Statistics confirm the crisis. Divorce in the U.S. peaked around 1980 at nearly 40% and has declined slightly since then. Still, roughly half of all marriages do not last. Secular wisdom often claims marriages collapse because of lost passion or excitement. In considering recent divorce statistics, researchers found the rate of divorce in the U.S. peaked at about 40% around 1980 and has been declining ever since. According to the National Survey of Family Growth, the probability of a first marriage lasting at least a decade was 68% for women and 70% for men between 2006 and 2010. The likelihood that they would make it 20 years was 52% for women and 56% for men, so that percentage is closer to the frequently-cited idea that "half of all marriages end in divorce."[2] Even more tragic, research indicates that one divorce occurs every 13 seconds here in the United States, ranking our nation sixth on a global divorce rate scale.[3]

The Biblical Root: Lack of Love

From a biblical perspective, marriages end in divorce because couples do not understand the purpose of marriage and their roles as husband and wife. They experience poor communication and have unresolved conflicts. We all desire passion and excitement in our marriages. Some people will use "the lack of passion and excitement" in their marriage to justify having an affair! But the lack of passion and excitement in marriages is not the cause of divorce. They are merely occasions that could lead to divorce. The point is that the biblical cause of divorce is considerably different from the presuppositions derived from human or secular wisdom.

The Biblical cause of divorce is the lack of love. Consider the following passage:

> So, as those who have been chosen of God, holy and beloved, put on a heart of compassion, kindness, humility, gentleness, and patience; bearing with one another, and forgiving each other, whoever has a complaint against anyone; just as the Lord forgave you, so also should you. Beyond all these things *put on* love, which is the perfect bond of unity. Let the peace of Christ rule in your hearts, to which indeed you were called in one body; and be thankful. (**Colossians 3:12-15**)

In Colossians 3:12-15, Paul identifies his audience as those who have been chosen by God. Every believer is in Christ. Paul says those chosen of God are also "holy" and "beloved." Holy means to be set apart and sanctified. What does this have to do with marriage?

God ordained marriage. It is a holy and beloved covenant between a man and a woman. God designed and sanctified marriage, setting it apart to reflect His image. His image is one of holiness and the unity of the Godhead: God the Father, Son, and Holy Spirit. God chose us to have an intimate relationship with Him and others, particularly our wives.

Paul goes on to say that, as those who are chosen, set apart, sanctified, and purified by the blood of Christ, we need to clothe ourselves with certain attitudes and behaviors. Since man and woman are created in God's Image, it is not a coincidence that the list of attributes Paul states in Colossians 3:12-14 are character traits that reflect Jesus Christ. Paul says, "Because we are chosen of God, we are to *put on* a heart of compassion."

To "*put on*" means to clothe yourself. You and I put on clothing every day. At least, I hope so! If you are attending a formal black-tie event, you wear formal attire. You clothe yourself to go to the gym to exercise. You put on clothing designed for working out and sweating. If you are a golfer, it is customary to clothe yourself in golfing attire before heading out of the house for a scheduled tee time. Paul says you must clothe yourself with the character of Christ, since God has chosen you. This is what those whom God selects are supposed to do.

Paul says Believers are to put on a heart of something. From a biblical perspective, the heart is the seat of a person's thoughts, emotions, feelings, impulses, passions, desires, and affections.[4]

Here is a definition of the heart:

> "The heart is the true inner self, rarely the physical organ. It is with the heart that a man feels, perceives, and makes moral choices. It is also with the heart that one seeks and responds to God. As the organ of moral choice, the heart is instinctively inclined toward evil, prompts action, is deceitful, and devises injustice."[5]

But Paul says, as one chosen by God, to clothe yourself, your thoughts, emotions, feelings, impulses, passions, desires, affections, and Will with a heart of compassion. The word "compassion" means to have mercy. Mercy means to withhold punishment from an offender who committed a wrong. Second, Paul says to put on a heart of kindness. Kindness means doing good, being generous, and being gracious to others. Third, Paul instructs us to put on humility, which entails exhibiting a lowly spirit with a heart of thanksgiving for all things, acknowledging that we are undeserving of God's grace and mercy. Humility compels you to meet the needs of others through service and sacrifice.

Fourth, Paul says, "put on a heart of gentleness and patience." As you can see, gentleness and patience are listed together. Gentleness is the willingness to suffer injury or insult rather than inflict such hurts. Gentleness connotes meekness, being mild-mannered, and considerate of others' well-being.[6] The word patience refers to bearing up under the irritating or disturbing behaviors of others without becoming annoyed or angry. Fifth, Paul says to put on a heart of "bearing with one another, and forgiving each other.". Forbearance means to bear up under provocation. It means tolerating and enduring injustice when others offend you with patience and without complaint. Forgiveness is about letting go of holding a grudge against a person for a wrong they have committed. When you forgive someone, it does not mean that the offense is forgotten, but rather that you choose not to hold a grudge against the person guilty of the offense. God's forgiveness towards you should compel you to forgive others as God has forgiven you.

Now Paul concludes this passage with the main point that summarizes the attributes that he listed in Colossians 3:12-13. He writes, *14 Beyond all these things put on love, which is the perfect bond of unity.* Every attribute that Paul listed is related to one's interpersonal relationships with others, which stem from one's relationship with God. Paul says that more important than any of these attributes, the essential garment of all to put on is a heart of love. The word "love" here is agape love. This kind of love is unconditional and cannot be earned. It is God's love. God's love is not contingent upon what a person has said or done. It is love with no strings attached. It is not based upon feelings but is a product of the will. Whether you feel like loving someone or not, "agape" love is something you choose to do.

Your love for others, particularly your wife, should not be based on what you get in return. There should be no hidden agenda or selfish motive. Unlike the world, true biblical love is always concerned with doing what is in the other person's best interest. Every attribute that the Apostle Paul lists in Colossians 3:12 through 14 is an expression of love. Why is love so important? Paul says it is the most important because it is the perfect bond of unity. Accordingly, love is the adhesive, the glue that holds marriages, people, and interpersonal relationships together in unity. Genesis 2:24 uses a similar word, which states; *Therefore shall a man leave his father and his mother, and shall **cleave** unto his wife: and they shall be one flesh.* Love compels the husband and wife to unite. It creates a waterproof relationship that endures the storms of life, opposition, and trials that can cause disunity in the marital relationship.

As I stated earlier, human wisdom may be partially correct in its conclusions that many marriages end in divorce due to decreased passion and a lack of excitement in the relationship. However, decreased passion and the lack of excitement in marriage are not the root cause of divorce. These things are merely symptoms of a bigger problem. The Biblical cause of divorce is the lack of love. Unloving attitudes of the heart cause disunity in the marriage.

When counseling married couples, I often have them read and memorize Colossians 3:12-14 as a homework assignment, using it as the foundation for marriage counseling. During the counseling session, I usually asked each of them if they felt there was a disconnect in their marriage. Why? Because if there is disunity in the marriage, it is likely because there is no love in the marriage; the adhesive that holds the marriage together is lacking. How do you know when there is no love in the marriage? What is the evidence of the lack of love in your marriage? Let us consider the list that Paul said concerning what God's chosen people must put on. As I help couples examine the condition of their marriage through the lens of Colossians 3:12-14, most of them make an interesting discovery. They quickly realize that instead of exhibiting a heart of compassion, they are exhibiting animosity and hatred towards one another. Instead of showing kindness, they are hostile and cruel towards one another. Instead of couples exhibiting humility, they are prideful and arrogant. Instead of showing gentleness and patience, they are harsh and impatient with one another. They are insensitive to one another's needs. Instead of couples bearing with one another and forgiving one another, they are intolerant of each other. They hold grudges, evidenced by their complaints against each other and refusal to forgive. There is no love because each person in the marriage is more concerned about themselves than their spouse.

Ironically, they were more concerned about one another when they were dating. In dating, they put the other person's desires and wants before their own. They demonstrated their love for one another by giving more and serving more. Now they are more concerned about what they are not getting in the marriage than what they are giving. They are now more concerned about being understood than being understanding. They are more concerned about receiving love than giving love. Even their search for passion and excitement in marriage is self-seeking and self-serving, driven by desires to please themselves. There is disunity in the marriage simply because there is no love.

Where is the love, and who is responsible for initiating it in the marriage? God is love, and a husband who loves God loves his wife. One's love for God indicates how much they love their wife. Love in marriage starts with the husband. The husband is commanded to love his wife as Christ loved the Church (Eph. 5:25-26). God holds husbands more responsible than wives for the condition of the marriage.

So why is loving our wives such a challenge at times? Loving our wives is challenging when we allow ourselves to be driven by selfish desires. We put on the wrong clothing. We refuse to clothe ourselves with a heart of love. We enable our wives' unfavorable responses to us to dictate how much we will love them. We love our wives based on what we get in return. It is not that we have no feelings of love for our wives, although that may be true for some. But biblical love is not based on emotions. It is not that we cannot love. Scriptures say, *for it is God who is at work in you, both to will and to work for His good pleasure.* **Philippians 2:12-13 (NASB)**

God does not command his children to do something without giving them the power to do so. As you can see, the Lord is at work in us for His good pleasure. The Holy Spirit dwells within us and empowers us to do what God commands us to do. We can choose to do what God calls us to or reject it. So, it is with our willingness or unwillingness to love our wives. Love is a choice. Most marriages end in divorce because husbands fail to love their wives. They consciously decide not to love—their refusal to love stems from their hearts' self-centered and wicked inclinations. The heart is only concerned about self-gratification. The heart is always asking: *What makes me happy? What do I want? What is in it for me? How have I been hurt and offended? What am I not getting?* The heart is like the stomach when it's hungry. No matter how often you fill it with good food, it always comes back the next day begging for more. Like the stomach, the heart is never satisfied. Nevertheless, you can have victory over the sinful inclinations of your heart. But How?

How Can a Husband Move from Unloving to Loving?

Many husbands, when faced with the challenges of loving their wives, respond by harboring bitterness and resentment. Yet, unloving attitudes, thoughts, and actions toward one's wife are sin. If you find yourself struggling with such unloving tendencies, the question becomes: How can you move from unloving to truly loving?

The apostle John lays out a clear biblical principle in 1 John 4:20–21:

> "If someone says, 'I love God,' and hates his brother, he is a liar; for the one who does not love his brother whom he has seen, cannot love God whom he has not seen. And this commandment we have from Him, that the one who loves God should love his brother also."

This passage applies directly to husbands when considered from another angle. Rephrased, it could read:

> "If a husband says, 'I love God,' but hates his wife, he is a liar; for the one who does not love his wife whom he has seen, cannot love God whom he has not seen. And this commandment we have from Him: the husband who loves God must also love his wife."

In other words, your love for your wife reflects your love for God. If you are guilty of sinning against your wife by failing to love her as Christ loved the church, how can you make it right—with God and with her?

Here are three biblical steps:

1. Confess your unloving attitudes, thoughts, words, and behaviors—both to God and to your wife.

2. Seek forgiveness from God and from your wife.

3. Repent by turning from your sin. Put off unloving responses and intentionally replace them with the attitudes, words, and actions that reflect the love of Christ. Romans 12:16-21 and Colossians 3:12-14 contain a multitude of loving Christlike responses that you can Put-On and practice.

True love requires dying to self, humility, repentance, and a daily commitment to reflect Christ's love in your marriage.

Here is the good news. A husband who chooses to love his wife will receive great rewards. A husband who loves his wife will find favor with God and enjoy His blessings. He will find inner peace and a clear conscience. A husband who loves his wife will reap the benefits of a wife who loves him in return. What compels a wife to respond to her husband lovingly? A wife will love her husband because she is grateful to have a husband who has pure motives. A wife will respect a husband who is peaceable, reasonable, full of mercy, and good fruits, without hypocrisy (James 3:15). All of the attributes describe the character of Christ. A husband who reflects the image of Christ in loving his wife will receive great rewards. So, how is genuine love defined, and what does it look like in practice? Let's start by examining what the love of Christ looks like in practice in the next chapter.

The question every husband must ask is: **Where is the love in my marriage?**

Not only "where is the love" but what defines love? We will define biblical love in the next chapter.

Reflection Questions

1. How does your current love for your wife compare to the love you showed when you were dating or newly married?

2. Which "garments" from Colossians 3:12–14 (compassion, kindness, humility, gentleness, patience, forgiveness) are weakest in your marriage right now?

3. In what ways has selfishness hindered your ability to love your wife sacrificially?

4. What step can you take this week to demonstrate unconditional, Christlike love to your wife?

Chapter 2
Love Defined
Loving Your Wife is a Choice

Childhood Love and Hard Lessons

I still remember my first "love." I was a ninth-grader in Houston, Texas, and smitten with a beautiful, brown-eyed girl in band class. Every morning, as I raised my trombone, I kept my eyes fixed on her. She was soft-spoken, wore a colorful scarf each day, and seemed innocent and sweet.

We talked on the phone every evening and met at a stairwell each morning before class. I even worked up the courage one day to give her a quick kiss on the lips — my very first. I thought it was the beginning of something lasting.

But one night, during one of our regular calls, she ended our relationship through a friend. My heart was crushed. I discovered the hard way what many of us learn young: the kind of "love" built only on feelings is fragile. It comes quickly, but it fades just as fast.

What's Good About Falling in Love?

There is a song entitled "Lovey Dovey," sung by musical artist and songwriter Tony Terry, that reached number four on the R&B charts in 1987. The song's lyrics describe the overwhelming feelings of love that a person experiences when they are with the one they love.

A myriad of popular love songs over the last few decades describe the pleasant feeling of being in love. Here are a few popular selections: "My Boo" by Alicia Keys and Usher, "I Believe in You and Me" by Whitney Houston, "Walking in the Rain with the One I Love" by Love Unlimited, and "My Girl" by the Temptations. All of these songs depict how most people define love today. The "Lovey Dovey" feelings of love are the common thread that connects all these famous love songs. Most people get married because of their "Lovey Dovey" feelings they get when they are with the person they love. But where do loving feelings begin? What role do feelings play in compelling people to get married? How is authentic love defined? Finally, can true love be measured by feelings?

Where Do Loving Feelings Begin?

Five elements of a romantic relationship include time, talking, trust, transparency, and touching. Love initially begins when two people enjoy spending time together and appreciate each other's company. Second, people develop loving feelings because they enjoy talking with one another. They have great conversations together that are effortless. They seem to have a lot in common and can talk about anything. They appear to connect. Some opposite sex co-workers enjoy talking with one another so much that they exchange phone numbers under the pretense of discussing work-related issues.

The third element that sparks feelings of love for someone is trust. Two people develop trust for one another as they spend time engaging in meaningful conversations. They understand one another, and as they devote more time to talking, they create trust. She seems to value his thoughts and is concerned about what he has to share. He believes that whatever he communicates to her is in safekeeping. She does not use what she knows about him or the information he has shared as a means to harm him. He has faith in her confidentiality and commitment. Does the development of mutual trust affect relationships? Absolutely! Trust plays a vital role in establishing intimacy.

The fourth element that ignites feelings of love between two people is transparency. Since they have developed confidence in one another, they become transparent. They are led to believe that the other person is no threat. There is no risk of danger in sharing their concerns. They become open with one another about their personal lives. So, they begin sharing their fears, goals, and private struggles. They listen intently and show genuine care and concern about one another's life stories. They both discover that they have more in common than they ever imagined regarding life experiences and life struggles.

Lastly, touching is the final ingredient for igniting romantic relationships. They have spent a lot of time together. They enjoy talking, and they seem to connect. They have developed a level of trust and are transparent with one another. Now, however subtle, they desire to make physical contact. The act of touching may begin with a pat on the back, a gentle touch/rub on the arm, or a friendly handshake. Touching may then escalate into hugging. Over time, the hugs become more frequent, longer, and more intense. One day, the fleeting thought of being physically intimate enters their minds, but may be quickly dismissed as a ludicrous idea. However, the idea of having sex with the other returns and begins to occur more and more frequently. The recurring thoughts seem to pop up out of nowhere. They may start to have dreams of engaging in sexual intercourse with one another. What was once a fleeting thought that each person initially dismissed has become a fantasy that they are now entertaining.

Finally, each individual began developing a strategic plan to make their fantasy a reality. Until finally, sexual intercourse consummates the relationship. Loving feelings are now driving the relationship. And the love songs, the vocals, and the melodies start to play in their hearts and minds. Who knows where or if it will end?

In some cases, relationships like this do not last. But in other situations, they manage to survive. The point is that relationships based on loving feelings alone cannot survive. Lasting relationships need Divine intervention to thrive. I stated five elements that ignite love as the World defines love. But is this true love? If not, how do you determine what real love is? And is the fact that you enjoy spending time together, talking, trusting, transparency, and touching one another justifiable reasons for getting married? Many couples get married based on loving feelings. People marry because the other person makes them feel secure, significant, and loved. But the question is, are loving feelings based on emotions alone, indicative of true love?

By the way, there is one caveat that I need to share with you regarding these five elements. These same five elements of loving feelings also ignite marital affairs and illicit sexual relationships. In this case, the outcome can be catastrophic, leading to the destruction of the marriage that extends beyond the individuals engaged in an illicit relationship.

Why do people get married?

Some people marry because the other person is meeting their felt needs. The most common reasons why people get married are to be happy, to find an identity, to have a purpose, to be loved and accepted, to achieve security, and to overcome loneliness.[1]

Some people get married because they want to be happy. Happiness is a state of well-being characterized by contentment, pleasure, and joy. However, sooner or later, these individuals experience disappointment in the marriage relationship because they realize that their partner does not always make them happy. When they are no longer happy in the marriage, they no longer have loving feelings for the person they married.

Other people get married in search of identity and purpose. They want to feel valued. Some people get married because they want validation. They can finally say, "I am somebody." Marriage provides meaning to their life.

Still, some get married because they have a need to be loved and accepted. When they feel loved and accepted, they have loving feelings. A few of these individuals may be searching for a parental type of love – a nurturing kind that they may not have received from their own parents. Some men want to marry a woman who resembles their ideal vision of a mother. Some women choose to marry men who resemble the perfect father. They want someone to fulfill what they did not receive as a child.

On the other hand, some have loving feelings because they believe the person they chose to marry has rescued them. He is her Knight in shining armor. Or a princess with a golden crown without a spot or wrinkle. They experience loving feelings for the person who loves them and accepts them unconditionally. These individuals view their selected mate as a kind of Savior.

Other people get married because they want security. Some people marry for emotional security, never to hurt again. Other people marry for financial security. As long as security is in place, they enjoy loving feelings for the other person. However, unforeseen situations, circumstances, and events are inevitable. Monetary problems are mundane. Couples will experience financial struggles. Sickness is unpredictable, and no one is exempt from a chronic illness that can wipe out a savings account.

Lastly, some people choose to get married to cure loneliness. They pursue marriage to heal loneliness and experience loving feelings stimulated by companionship. First, let's differentiate between being alone and loneliness. Some people can detach from others without stress; in other words, a person can be solitary and utterly content while alone. Introverts are loners. However, loneliness is an emotional state characterized by feelings of sadness or gloom resulting from the absence of close friends or intimate relationships. Solitude sometimes is indicative of depression.

Some people become lonely because they are widows. Many Divorcees also suffer from loneliness. For that reason, some divorcees make the mistake of remarrying far too soon before they have had a chance to heal emotionally and mentally from a prior divorce. The point is that some people get married as a means of curing loneliness.

Here are a few more critical questions about "loving feelings!" Are loving feelings, stimulated by fulfilling felt needs, indicative of true love? Should true love be predicated on what a person can get from marriage? Let's start by examining how the World defines true love in comparison to the Word of God.

How is Love Defined?

The World's View of Love - *Feelings and Felt Needs*

According to Human Wisdom, love is a fundamental human emotion. It is an intense desire for physical intimacy and contact with another person. Psychologists, Human Wisdom, and Secular counselors (titles I will use interchangeably) define love as a feeling. "It involves feelings of compassionate love that develop out of feelings of mutual respect and feelings of mutual understanding for one another. Passionate love can be described as intense emotions, sexual attraction, and affection. People are satisfied and fulfilled when the other person reciprocates these intense feelings. Unreciprocated love can lead to despondency and despair." [2]

Secular wisdom also asserts that a person learns how to love through their relationship with their mother. Some secular counselors believe that, from infancy, children learn how to love by imitating their parents. They assert that the purpose of true parental love is to provide security, thereby maximizing the child's growth. Secular wisdom suggests that true love must include communion in mutual sharing to satisfy each other's needs and the individuation of confidence and successful competition. Love must encompass mutuality and individuality, as well as the relationship with others and oneself.[3] Some psychologists embrace the erroneous presupposition that one cannot love others unless one first loves oneself. Secular wisdom believes that man must learn to love himself because *"unconditional love for self is essential to our growth and ...our well-being." In other words, it is the belief that a person cannot export what he has not imported.*[4]

Based on their definition of love, worldly wisdom suggests that decreased passion and a lack of excitement in marriage are the primary causes of most divorces. What's wrong with the World's view of love? The World's idea of love and why couples choose to part ways are based on loving feelings and felt needs. However, the biblical view of love differs from the secular view.

The Biblical View of Love - *a Reflection of God's Image*

The Bible commands believers to exhibit Agape love- unconditional love for God and others. Agape love is an attribute of God's nature. It is a reverence for and a deep acknowledgment of God's divine being, with thanksgiving. It is a love of God's word and commandments, as well as obedience to God's commands. God created man and woman in His image. God created marriage to reflect His image; that is God's purpose. Genesis 1: 26-27 says:

> Then God said, "Let Us make man in Our image, according to Our likeness; and let them rule over the fish of the sea and over the birds of the sky and over the cattle and over all the earth, and over every creeping thing that creeps on the earth." God created man in His own image, in the image of God He created him; male and female He created them.

God only shares His communicable attributes with man. God's communicable attributes include love, goodness, intellect, the ability to reason, volition, mercy, knowledge, and wisdom. But love is the greatest of all of God's communicable attributes. All of God's attributes stem from love. Consider the following passage.

> Beloved, let us *love* one another, for *love is from God*, and everyone who *loves* is born of God and knows God. The one who does not love does not know God, **for God is love**. By this, **the love of God** was manifested in us, that God has sent His only begotten Son into the World so that we might live through Him. In this is *love*, not that we loved God, but that **He loved**

us and sent His Son *to be* the propitiation for our sins. Beloved, **if God so loved us**, we also ought to **love** one another. (**1 John 4:7-11**)

Love is God's nature. Love is from God. The nature of ice is cold. The nature of water is wet. The nature of fire is hot. Comparably, the nature of God is love. First John 4:7-11 says that love is from God. Those who have a relationship and are in fellowship with God also love as God loves. Most children usually adopt some of their parents' character traits and mannerisms. When we love others (particularly our wives) as God loves us, we essentially reflect our heavenly Father's character. God's gracious and sacrificial act of love allows a sinner (as ourselves) to come to know and love God. However, there is a caveat! It is impossible to love, as defined by the Bible and not Human wisdom, apart from God. A person who does not love does not know God. And if he claims to know God but does not love, his unwillingness to love may result from blatant disobedience or a failure to walk by faith in fellowship with God. Love involves attitude and deliberate action.

Moreover, Biblical love is unconditional; it has no strings attached. There are no limits to biblical love. From a Biblical perspective, love is not based on feelings or felt needs. Agape love is not just based on talking, time, trust, transparency, and physical touch with another person. Agape love stems from time spent in conversation, trust, transparency, and pursuing intimacy with God, our Lord and Savior, Jesus Christ. It is a love not based on what one gets in return. Agape love is not contingent on another person fulfilling your felt needs, such as a need to be happy, to find an identity, to have a purpose, to be loved and accepted, to have security, and to cure loneliness. God's love alone is fulfilling. God's love makes us joyful (not necessarily happy but content and thankful). God's love provides us with identity, gives us purpose, and compels us to embrace His love and acceptance of us (Romans 8:28-30, 38-39, 2 Cor. 5:9, 1 John 4:18-19). By God's love, we are sealed with eternal security (Eph. 1:13). Agape is a cure for loneliness because it compels us to draw closer to God and others (Psalms 3, 13, 17, 25). Biblical love is gracious and undeserving.

Genuine love is giving yourself, your talents, your time, and your treasures to benefit another (specifically your wife) and expecting nothing in return (Luke 6:30-36).

Are Loving Feelings indicative of Genuine Love or a Counterfeit?

In 2005, my wife and I, along with a few other married couples, took a romantic getaway to Manhattan, New York. On one occasion, we stopped in front of a storefront, where a small, petite saleswoman stood, trying to entice our wives into buying a purse. The purses were quite expensive. The saleslady struggled to convince our wives to make the purchase. Suddenly, the saleslady said something that instantly caught the attention of our wives. She said, *"I have something inside the back of the store that I think may capture your interest. I have a few Gucci and Louis Vuitton purses for a discounted price."* Our wives started talking to one another simultaneously (something about women I still do not fully understand) and hurriedly followed the saleswoman to the back of the store. They examined the merchandise. The Seams on the purses looked good. The logos on the merchandise appeared to be straight and spelled correctly. However, the leather smelled strange, like glue, rubber, or chemicals, rather than genuine leather. These bags typically retail for $800 or $1,200.

The saleswoman offered them an unbelievable price of $100 or $200, depending on the purse. WOW! What a deal! Our wives stepped away from the saleswoman for a moment of privacy and formed a huddle to discuss whether they should make a purchase. But something about the deal did not seem right with a few of them. Finally, they declined the offer, and we continued on our way. It was the best decision our wives made on the entire trip. Why? Because we found out afterwards that the purses were possibly counterfeit. On our way back to the hotel, we shared our shopping experience with the cab driver who drove us back. He told us about the infestation of counterfeiters who set up shop in New York, whose sole purpose is to deceive and take advantage of tourists. The counterfeit purses appeared to be genuine but were actually fake.

What is a counterfeit? A counterfeit is an imitation of the real thing. Counterfeit products are unauthorized replicas of authentic products. Counterfeit products are produced with the intent to take advantage of the superior value of the imitated product.[5]

When it comes to love, how can you distinguish the genuine from the counterfeit? True love is not about what one receives from another person but what one can give. Real love is not based upon personal benefits but stems from loving God. Your love for your wife is indicative of your love for God. But love, as defined by the world, is a counterfeit.

First, the World's definition of love is counterfeit because Secular wisdom asserts that love is based solely on human emotion. True love is not based solely on feelings, although emotions are often a significant part of it. However, biblical love is not exclusively based on emotions and feelings, but on caring attitudes and actions, regardless of one's feelings.

Second, the World's definition of love is counterfeit because Secular wisdom claims that a person learns how to love through their relationship with their mother. However, the Bible declares that true love comes from God, not one's parents (1 John 4:7). While it is true that mothers and fathers have a tremendous influence on a child's life, they are not the determining factor in whether a child grows up to become a loving adult. Secular wisdom or psychology asserts that a person's ability to love is determined by the quality and quantity of love he received from his mother. The idea is that if a person is unloving, it is the parent's fault, not his own. Therefore, he cannot be held accountable for unloving attitudes and actions towards others.

However, according to the Word of God, we are all held responsible for loving God and others. It is a commandment. Matthew 22:36-40 says,

> "Teacher, which is the great commandment in the Law?" And He said to him, " 'YOU SHALL LOVE THE LORD YOUR GOD WITH ALL YOUR HEART, AND WITH ALL YOUR SOUL, AND WITH ALL YOUR MIND.' "This is the great and foremost commandment. "The second is like it,

'YOU SHALL LOVE YOUR NEIGHBOR AS YOURSELF.'
"On these two commandments depend the whole Law and the
Prophets."

According to the gospel of Matthew, love has nothing to do with your genet-
ics or how your parents raised you. Nor is it contingent upon your environment.
Your ability to love has everything to do with your love for God. The quality
and quantity of your love for others is a mirror reflection of how much you love
God.

Third, the World's definition of love is counterfeit because Secular wisdom
suggests that true love must include "communion in the mutual sharing to
satisfy each other's needs and individuation of confidence and successful competition." In other words, Secular belief is that people experience true love
when they mutually share in meeting one another's needs. True love stems from
having self-confidence and the ability to outdo others in pursuit of personal
recognition and reward. The secular idea is that true love must involve giving
and taking in relationships with others, coupled with individual self-confidence,
self-worth, and being acknowledged by others. In contrast to this idea, the
Bible declares that love based on mutual sharing, giving, satisfying one another's needs, and promoting self-esteem and self-worth is of the World (1 John
2:15-17).

Fourth, the World's definition of love is counterfeit because Secular wisdom
embraces the erroneous presupposition that one cannot love others if one does
not love oneself first. However, the Bible affirms that humans naturally and
instinctively love themselves. In Mathew 22: 37-39, Jesus said that the Greatest
commandment is to love God, and the second is to love your neighbor as
yourself. Jesus says we must love our neighbor as we already love ourselves. The
ability to love comes from God. He gave it to us. God commands us to love, and
in doing so, we are demonstrating the essence of His character.

When you love your wife, you are merely loving her the way God loves you.
You are giving back what God has given you. So, the idea that you cannot love

if you don't have it within yourself to give is a false assumption. Consider this passage:

> So husbands ought also to love their own wives as their own bodies. He who loves his own wife loves himself; for no one ever hated his own flesh, but nourishes and cherishes it, just as Christ also *does* the church, **Ephesians 5:28-29 (NASB)**

The problem for many of us is that we love ourselves far too much. Sure, we love our neighbors. But sometimes, the neighbor whom we love is ourselves! If a person says they do not love themselves, I would ask, "Why are you still feeding, clothing, and caring for yourself?" As we just read in Ephesians 5:28-29, no man ever hated himself but nourishes and cherishes himself.

Furthermore, 2 Timothy 3:1-3 says,

> But realize this, that in the last days difficult times will come. For men will be lovers of self, lovers of money, boastful, arrogant, revilers, disobedient to parents, ungrateful, unholy, unloving, irreconcilable, malicious gossips, without self-control, brutal, haters of good,

As I stated, the Bible declares that love based on mutual sharing, giving, satisfying one another's needs, and promoting self-esteem and self-worth are of the World (1 John 2:15-17). The Bible gives a clear warning against loving in this way;

> Do not love the World nor the things in the World. If anyone loves the World, the love of the Father is not in him. For all that is in the World, the lust of the flesh and the lust of the eyes and the boastful pride of life is not from the Father but is from the

World. The World is passing away, and also its lusts, but the one who does the will of God lives forever. (**1 John 2:15-17**)

In light of 1 John 2:15-17, the writer warns against loving the World because the World and the things that we burn for that are of the World are passing away, and loving like the World only brings momentary satisfaction. If you love your wife based on the mutual sharing in meeting one another's emotional needs, then your love for her is based on the lust of the flesh. If you love your wife based on self-confidence and a desire for personal recognition and reward, you love your wife according to the pride of life. Some people want to be viewed as competent, successful, and valued by others. However, if these things are the driving forces behind your love for your wife, then you love her based on your cravings for glory and selfish desire to be esteemed—those in the World love one another in this way.

If your love for your wife is based on tangible things she gives or does for you, then your love for her is of the World because it is motivated by the lust of the eyes. It is driven by things that you want from her. What do you want from your wife? Do you want her to cook? Clean? Do you want her to give you as much sex as often as you want? Do you want her approval for a new purchase of a car, boat, and motorcycle? There is nothing wrong with wanting these things. However, if your love for her is driven by what she does for or gives to you, then your love for her is driven by lust.

One's passion is based on feelings. A person's excitement is based on being entertained. From the World's perspective, love is based upon how a person feels about the other person, how they think about themselves, and what they get in return.

Allow me to illustrate the point. Most stockholders invest in the stock market because they anticipate a return on their investment. If the market falls below expectations, that could mean risking a loss on their investment. So they sell the poor-performing stock that does nothing for them, buy mutual funds where their money is protected, or get out of the market altogether. What does this have to do with marriage? People bail out of marriages because they are not getting a return on their investment. The marriage relationship has fallen below expectations. So, they shut down to protect themselves. Or they get out of the relationship through an adulterous relationship or bail out in a divorce. Secular wisdom suggests that a decrease in passion and a lack of excitement in marriage are the primary causes of most divorces. Still, the truth is that marriages end in divorce because people feel they have taken a loss on their marital investment, so they refuse to continue contributing to the relationship. In other words, they chose not to love as God defines love.

Loving Like Christ is a Daily Choice.

Loving your wife is a conscious, everyday decision. Feelings feel real, but they aren't dependable. They come and go depending on mood, stress, circumstances, or situations. If your marriage is dependent on feelings alone, it will drift during storms. But when love is a choice — grounded in God's command and Christ's example — it becomes steady and unshakable. When feelings fade, love stays. When frustrations grow, love persists. When offenses happen, love forgives. Each day, you face a choice. My challenge is for you to take a moment each day and ask yourself, "What is one thing I can do today to show love for my wife like Christ loved the church, no matter how I feel?"

Practical Implications for Husbands

1. Stop Waiting to Feel Love — Start Choosing It.

Do something kind for your wife even when you don't "feel" like it. Obedience often leads to renewed affection.

2. Anchor Your Love in God's Word, Not Your Emotions.

Meditate on passages like 1 Corinthians 13 and Ephesians 5. Let Scripture reshape your understanding of love.

3. See Love as Sacrifice, Not Transaction.

Love isn't about what you get, but what you give. Christ's love was selfless and sacrificial.

4. Pray for God's Help to Love Beyond Yourself.

You cannot love your wife this way in your own strength. Rely on the Holy Spirit for patience, humility, and perseverance.

Conclusion

The biblical perspective of true love involves acts of giving to another person, expecting nothing in return (Luke 6 32-36). Genuine love requires humility and not self-esteem or self-worth. True love does not seek public recognition or approval. It is not motivated by selfish ambition but is driven by seeing others as more important than yourself (Rom. 12:3-4; Phil. 2:3-4). You chose to love your wife even when there are no loving feelings. It is choosing to love your wife when your felt needs are unmet. It involves loving your wife even when she is offensive and undeserving. Loving your wife requires sacrifice. When you make a deliberate decision to love your wife, then feelings will follow.

The World defines love as a fleeting feeling. But God defines love as a deliberate choice, expressed through patience, kindness, sacrifice, and endurance.

Husbands, your calling is not to love your wife only when it feels easy, but to love her as Christ loved the church — faithfully, sacrificially, and unconditionally.

Love is not something you fall into. It's something you put on — every single day.

While it is true that you cannot buy love, the truth is that love bought you. You and I were purchased for a price. So why should you love your wife? Because you were purchased by the Blood of Jesus Christ that was shed on the cross for the penalty of your sin. Scripture says:

- But God demonstrates His own love toward us, in that while we were yet sinners, Christ died for us. **Romans 5:8**

- In this is love, not that we loved God, but that He loved us and sent His Son *to be* the propitiation for our sins. **1 John 4:10 (NASB)**

As such, we are no longer our own. We are God's possession. God is Love. As such, He is the source of true love. Loving your wife is a commandment from

God. But you may ask, *"How can I love my wife when she refuses to love me back?"* I'm glad you asked! We'll discuss how to overcome the challenges of loving your wife in the following chapters.

Reflection Questions

1. When you look at your marriage, how much of your love has been based on feelings versus deliberate choices?

2. Which description of biblical love in 1 Corinthians 13:4-7 do you most need to strengthen in your relationship

3. How can you begin showing love this week as an act of obedience, even when emotions are weak?

4. What daily prayer can you begin using to ask God to help you love your wife like Christ loved the church?

Chapter 3

Loving Your Wife Even When Love is Not Returned

Love Based Upon Even Exchange

When I was in grade school, my brother and I had a tradition every Halloween. After a long night of trick-or-treating, we would come home, dump out our bags of candy, and combine them into one big pile on the table. Then came the fun part—we would take turns picking our favorites. We called it the "one-for-one rule."

He would choose one piece, place it on his side of the table, and then it was my turn to choose. Back and forth we went, carefully selecting, trading evenly, and enjoying the game.

At first, it worked perfectly. However, as the pile shrank, the choices became increasingly difficult. The cheap candies—peppermints, tootsie rolls, jellybeans, caramels, and those dreaded sugar-coated orange slices—were plentiful. But the prized candies, the ones everyone wanted—Snickers, Butterfingers, Baby Ruths, Almond Joys, Three Musketeers, and Milk Duds—were disappearing fast.

Then came the turning point. I spotted and grabbed the very last Reese's Peanut Butter Cup. Suddenly, the rules changed. My brother declared that since I had taken the last of the best candy, the "one-for-one" rule no longer applied. Now it was two-for-one. Fair exchange was gone, and the balance of our little candy economy collapsed.

What followed was predictable: the game ended, and a candy war began. My brother and I became adversaries that Halloween night, sitting across from each other with our stashes, refusing to share. Yet no matter how angry we were, there was one truth we couldn't escape—adversaries or not, we still lived under the same roof. We were giving based on what we received in return.

We were not only brothers, but neighbors who could not part ways.

It reminded me later of Jesus' words in Matthew 22:37-39: "Love the Lord your God with all your heart and with all your soul and with all your mind. This is the first and greatest commandment. And the second is like it: Love your neighbor as yourself."

Your wife is your closest neighbor. But what do you do when the love you show your wife is not reciprocated? To truly love your wife, you must give love as you hope to receive, even when the rules seem unfair.

The Problem with Loving as the World Loves

What caused my brother and me to become adversaries? What is at the root of our unloving attitudes and actions towards one another? Is it simply about candy sections, or is there something else? The fact is, we were being selfish. We were showing love for one another based on how it could benefit us personally. We were willing to love only if we received love in return. We were willing to do good to one another based on receiving good. We were willing to give to one another based on what we received in return.

In fact, consider how the world loves, and the one-for-one rule for loving, doing good, and lending to those who reciprocate the same in return is a way of life. It manifests in various settings, including our government, the legal system, prisons, among coworkers, with our bosses, and within family members.

Politicians will make promises. Some politicians promise to do good, grant monetary favors, and lend support in exchange for receiving votes to win an election. It is sad, but the rule of loving based on even exchange may even show up in some churches. I know of a member of a particular church who was in dire need of assistance. However, when they reached out to the church where they were active members, they were denied help because, although they had given money to the church, they were not considered true tithers. They were told by a church administrator, *"Sorry, we can't help you."* The administrator's words broke their hearts! But that is how the World loves, that is to "love those who love."

The World's Way of Loving

What is the World's Golden Rule for loving others, including your enemies? Jesus said, "You have heard that it was said, 'YOU SHALL LOVE YOUR NEIGHBOR and hate your enemy.' **(Matt. 5:43)**

What is the source of love that Jesus is speaking of in Mathew 5:43? The kind of love that Jesus is referring to is rooted in the sinful nature of man! The natural man is instinctively a sinner by nature. The heart of man is instinctively concerned only about self, and it wants. Mark 7:20-23 says,

> And He [Jesus] was saying, "That which proceeds out of the man, that is what defiles the man. For from within, out of the heart of men, proceed the evil thoughts, fornications, thefts, murders, adulteries, deeds of coveting and wickedness, as well as deceit, sensuality, envy, slander, pride, and foolishness. All these evil things proceed from within and defile the man."

Notice what Jesus says about the nature of the heart and how it directs man's thoughts and behavior. Jesus says the desires of the human heart give birth to one's thoughts, and thoughts give birth to action. The heart says, "me, me, me, me." It is never satisfied. The heart compels a person to do for others with the expectation of receiving something of equal or greater value in return.

Is There Something Wrong with a Husband's Desire to be loved by His Wife?

A husband's desire to receive love from his wife is neutral. But to withhold love from your wife because you are getting nothing in return is sinful. Do you know that when it comes to loving others, those in the world think the same way? The World embraces this mindset. *"Love those who love you."* The natural inclination of the human heart is to be concerned only about self-gratification. As I stated in the previous chapter, the Bible defines the heart as the inner control center of the affections, reasoning, emotions, desires, and the will. The heart is always asking, *What's in it for me?*

What's Wrong With Loving Your Wife Based on What You Get in Return?

Loving others who love you in return is often referred to as "conditional love." In Luke 6:32-36, the writer of this gospel offers a glimpse into how the world loves, as expressed through acts of kindness and generosity. In Luke 6:32-34, Jesus says

> "If you **love** those who love you, what credit is that to you? For even sinners love those who love them. "If you **do good** to those who do good to you, what credit is that to you? For even sinners do the same. "If you **lend** to those from whom you expect to receive, what credit is that to you? Even sinners lend to sinners in order to receive back the same amount.

Jesus states that true love involves loving, doing good, and giving to others in need, but sinners do these things based on what they get in return. Jesus says to His disciples, "If you love others, do good, and lend to others based on the one-for-one rule, you are no better than sinners who reject me."

Previously, in Luke 6:27-28, Luke records Jesus' conversation with His disciples about loving their enemies. Jesus said, *But I say to you who hear, love your enemies, do good to those who hate you, bless those who curse you, pray for those who mistreat you.*

As Jesus is having this conversation with His disciples, He reiterates, in verses 6:35-36, not only the need to love your enemy, but also states the reason and the rewards of doing so. Jesus said, *And your reward will be great, and you will be sons of the Most High; for He Himself is kind to ungrateful and evil men. Be merciful, just as your Father is merciful.*

Jesus told the disciples that they should not love, to be good, and lend as the World does, expecting to receive in return. Jesus says his disciples are called to love differently from those of the world. They were part of the Kingdom of God. The disciples were chosen by Jesus to have a relationship with the Father and to follow Him. In the Kingdom of God, loving others based on the one-for-rule violates God's command. Unconditional love is unbecoming of those who are in Christ and distorts God's character.

First, Jesus says, "You should love your enemies." But how does biblical love look? Scripture says in Colossians 3:12-14:

> So, as those who have been chosen of God, holy and beloved, put on a heart of compassion, kindness, humility, gentleness, and patience; bearing with one another, and forgiving each other, whoever has a complaint against anyone; just as the Lord forgave you, so also should you. Beyond all these things, *put on* love, which is the perfect bond of unity.

As one who has been chosen of God, you possess the power, through the indwelling of the Holy Spirit, to put on a heart of unconditional love for your wife. To love your wife is to have a heart of compassion by being sensitive to her needs. Loving your wife means showing her kindness by being considerate of her concerns and feelings. Loving your wife also requires humility. A humble person always sees others as more important than himself. There can be no true love without humility. Why? Because love involves humility, which in turn compels you to make sacrifices for the benefit of your wife. And sacrifice is expressed in giving to others. Gentleness is another characteristic of love. Gentleness is not arrogant, harsh, or cruel. A gentle person has a calm and soothing disposition. Gentleness also involves being softhearted, compassionate, merciful, and sympathetic when dealing with your wife. Love also requires patience, which means being long-suffering and self-restraining. Long-suffering is the ability to endure when your wife has injured you. It is the ability to endure provocation for extended periods without retaliating. It is the ability to exhibit self-control in the face of provocation. Love means to exhibit forbearance, or to bear with others. Forbearance means to tolerate your wife's imperfections and shortcomings. A husband who loves in this manner does not become irritated with her. In essence, the term *"to bear with"* means to put up with; to tolerate. Love also means to forgive others. To forgive does not mean that the offense is forgotten; it means that the offense is forgiven. But it does mean that the forgiver chooses not to hold a grudge against the offender. Forgiveness is a choice. True love does not blame-shift. A loving husband examines himself, even when he is offended, and takes responsibility for his own contribution and unloving response to a particular problem. He does so by pondering the question, "Where am I wrong in this?" He identifies his sin, confesses it to God, seeks God's forgiveness, and also seeks the forgiveness of the one he sinned against. And if the offender is genuinely wrong, then forgive her. But why, and to what extent, should you forgive? Remember, Jesus said that there is no credit, no rewards, for loving your wife based upon what you get in return. Not only should you love your wife, but you are also to do good to her, expecting nothing in return.

Example of Doing Good

Second, Jesus says, ^{33} *"Do good ..."* Doing good to others is another expression of love.

Goodwill was founded in 1902 in Boston by Rev. Edgar J. Helms, a Methodist minister and visionary social innovator. Helms began with a simple yet powerful idea: he collected used household goods and clothing from wealthier neighborhoods, then trained and hired those living in poverty to repair and restore them. The items were either resold or given directly to the very people who had renewed them. Out of this exchange, the Goodwill philosophy of offering "a hand up, not a handout" was born.

Dr. Helms' vision laid the foundation for what is now a $5 billion nonprofit organization. He described Goodwill Industries as "an industrial program as well as a social service enterprise... a provider of employment, training, and rehabilitation for people of limited employability, and a source of temporary assistance for individuals whose resources were depleted."

Though times have changed, Helms' mission continues to resonate. He once declared, "We have courage and are unafraid. With the prayerful cooperation of millions of our bag contributors and of our workers, we will press on till the curse of poverty and exploitation is banished from mankind."

Carrying that vision forward, Goodwill Industries of Colorado Springs recently celebrated its Annual Dinner on April 13, honoring outstanding businesses and individuals while unveiling its new slogan: "Work to Improve Lives."

Indeed, Goodwill has done—and continues to do—remarkable work in meeting the needs of people worldwide. Their impact is evident not only in their programs but in the testimony of countless individuals whose lives have been touched by their generosity and opportunities. Goodwill, in its very name, embodies the act of doing good.

Yet this naturally raises a deeper question: what does it mean "to do good" as a husband from a biblical perspective? Scripture teaches that to "do good" is to show mercy to your wife, to act with kindness, to help her when she is in need, to do what is right, and to embody compassion. In this way, Goodwill is more than an organization—it reflects a timeless calling for husbands to live out goodness in action, extending love and dignity to our wives and others around us.

The word of God says,

- **Psalms 34:8,** O taste and see that the LORD is good; How blessed is the man who takes refuge in Him!

- **Psalms 100:5,** For the LORD is good; His lovingkindness is everlasting, and His faithfulness to all generations.

- **Psalms 145:9,** The LORD is good to all, and His mercies are over all His works.

Goodness is an expression of love. Doing good to your wife means that you have a heart of compassion, grace, mercy, lovingkindness, faithfulness, forgiveness, and righteousness towards her (Col. 3:12-14). You are to exhibit goodness, not only in terms of your heart but also in terms of how you relate to her. Doing good also implies granting favors with the intention of helping your wife according to her immediate need. But why, and to what extent, should you do good to your wife? To the same extent that God has been good to you! When you love your wife in this manner, it is the conduit for overcoming evil schemes of Satan designed to destroy your marriage relationship. It establishes unity in the relationship. There is a great reward for doing good for your wife. It creates peace, guards against contention, and forgives all faults. But there is no credit, no rewards, for doing good to her based upon what you get in return.

Third, Jesus also says, "*If you Lend*...." Lending to others is the final expression of love that Jesus mentions in Luke 3:27-36. But what does Jesus mean by the term *"lend?"* In the Old Testament, the idea of lending meant to be generous and freely give to others in need without expecting anything in return. In the Old Testament, lending and borrowing went hand in hand because the lender lends to the legitimate needs of the borrower, who is the person in need. King Solomon wrote;

^{17} He who is kind to the poor lends to the LORD, and he will reward him for what he has done. **Proverbs 19:17 (NIV)**

What is interesting is that the ability to lend came from God's abundant material blessings to the Children of Israel. As a result, if the Children of Israel refused to lend to those in need, they were in direct violation of God's Law.

In the New Testament, the concept of lending, among God's people, differed slightly from that of the Old Testament. Jesus tells the disciples to lend to others in need, expecting nothing in return. Lending to others in need is a display of generosity, compassion, and grace.

Illustration

I remember when we purchased our first home. Like most couples, we couldn't afford to pay cash, so we applied for a mortgage loan with a bank. In other words, we had to find a lender. Banks, of course, are in the business of lending. Whether it's a mortgage, a home equity loan, an auto loan, a payday loan, or even a credit card cash advance, the principle is the same: the bank is the lender, and consumers are the borrowers. At the closing table, the lender provides the funds, allowing the borrower to complete the purchase. Both parties then sign the mortgage note, a promissory document that secures the agreement. The note serves as evidence of the borrower's debt and obligation to repay—not only the original amount borrowed but also the interest.

And because banks operate for profit, they add yet another layer of security: a lien on the property. If the borrower fails to keep their repayment obligation, the lender can take possession of the property to protect itself from loss. At its core, lending in this world is always tied to return, interest, and gain.

But in Luke 6:35, Jesus calls us to a very different standard: "But love your enemies, and do good, and lend, expecting nothing in return. Then your reward will be great, and you will be children of the Most High..."

This principle is not limited to strangers or outsiders—it applies most intimately to a husband as he seeks to love his wife. For example, there is a great reward when a husband "lends" to his wife, expecting nothing in return. And lending doesn't always mean money. It may mean lending her your time, patience, encouragement, forgiveness, or even a listening ear. Unlike a bank, the husband's love is not transactional. He does not keep a ledger of debts or demand interest on every sacrifice he has made.

Instead, he gives freely, motivated by love and obedience to God. And in that kind of lending—expecting nothing back—the true interest is paid not in dollars, but in deeper trust, unity, and blessing within the marriage.

What is the Credit for Love?

Jesus says, if you love, do good, and lend to those who do the same for you, there is no credit for loving others in this way. The word "Credit" refers to Grace, unmerited favor, Goodwill, and kindness. Credit is also quite similar to the gratuity that servers receive in restaurants. Generally, most people appreciate going to a restaurant where the food is good and the service is excellent. Usually, people leave a tip or credit their waiter as a token of appreciation and thanks. But Jesus says that there is no reward, gratuity, tip, or credit for loving, doing good, and lending, expecting to receive in return.

Is the love you give your wife less than what you receive in return? Has she failed to meet your expectations? Is there a possibility that there may be some internal issues that you have not considered? Your wife may have an internal problem, such as bitterness, resentment, and/or unforgiving, unloving attitudes towards you, that she may be entertaining. The problem may be sin. Yet it is during those times that she needs you to love her most. She needs your grace and mercy. Be mindful that you both are sinners who said, "I Do." In fact, sin may also be your problem. What I mean is, the same bitterness, resentment, or unforgiving, unloving attitudes that she has towards you may be the same attitudes you may have towards her in response to her not loving you in return. So give her credit. Show her favor. Identify her need and love her, expecting nothing in return. Do you desire for God to love you in the same way? So, love your wife the way God loves you.

What Credit Does God Give You for Loving Your Wife?

God's mercy and an abundance of blessings are the credits you receive for loving your wife. In Luke 6, Jesus gives a reason why we should love, do good, and lead, expecting nothing in return. He said.

> "But love your enemies, do good to them, and lend to them without expecting to get anything back. *Then your reward will be great, and you will be children of the Most High, because he is kind to the ungrateful and wicked. Be merciful, just as your Father is merciful.* (Luke 6:35-36)

Jesus said, "Your reward will be great." God will reward you for loving your wife. Mercy is an expression of love. When you show mercy, you reflect the image of your heavenly Father, who is merciful and kind to ungrateful and evil men. Just as we all once were and still are at times. Loving your wife is an act of mercy. But what does mercy look like in practice? Jesus tells us what mercy looks like when he said,

> "Do not judge, and you will not be judged. Do not condemn, and you will not be condemned. Forgive, and you will be forgiven. [38] Give, and it will be given to you. A good measure, pressed down, shaken together, and running over, will be poured into your lap. For with the measure you use, it will be measured to you."

Jesus says that you show mercy towards your wife by not judging her.

For clarification, we are called to exercise righteous judgment. Righteous judgment always involves condemning injustice in the world. We can also exercise righteous judgment by confronting sin and using compassionate correction to restore those who are guilty. However, the judgment that Jesus is warning against is not righteous judgment but human judgment. Human judgment involves condemning and punishing the guilty for the wrongs they committed. Jesus says that we are not to exercise human judgment. Instead, Jesus says we are to forgive one another. How does forgiveness apply to you as a husband?

To the same degree in which you are forgiving and merciful towards your wife is the same degree in which God will be forgiving and merciful towards you. In doing so, your rewards will be overflowing, pressed down, and shaken together (Lk. 6:37-38). The following is a list of other practical ways you can be merciful towards your wife.

Practical Ways to Love When It's Hard

1. **Pray for God's Strength** – Ask God to soften your heart and renew your capacity to love. Loving unconditionally is not natural - it requires the Spirit of God.

2. **Serve Without Strings Attached** – Do small, intentional acts of kindness without expecting a thank you or reciprocation. This resets your heart to love freely.

3. **Guard Against Resentment** – Bitterness is poison. Refuse to rehearse wrongs. Instead, forgive daily, just as Christ forgives you.

4. **Speak Life, Not Criticism** – Words shape the atmosphere of your marriage. Replace complaints with encouragement, even if your wife does not return it.

5. **Stay Anchored in God's Word** – Scripture reminds you that your marriage is ultimately about reflecting Christ. Keep your eyes on Him when your wife's responses discourage you.

Godly Love is Not Based on the One-for-One Rule

The one-for-one rule does not apply to loving others as a child of God. What if God's love for you were based on the one-for-one rule? Although His love for us is much greater than our love for Him, especially in view of what Christ did on the Cross, God would be on the short receiving end of the stick. Yet, even though our love for Him pales in comparison to His love for us, He continues to show love for us even when it is not reciprocated. He still chooses to love us; to have mercy upon us, and He continues to cover us with His amazing grace. Is there a limit to God's love for us? He loves us so much that no matter how much we offend Him, He is still willing to forgive us if we confess and repent of our sins. God's love for us does not exempt us from His discipline. Even God's discipline of us is an expression of His unconditional love for us.

> *My child, don't ignore it when the LORD disciplines you, and don't be discouraged when he corrects you. For the LORD corrects those he loves, just as a father corrects a child in whom he delights.*
> **Proverbs 3:11-12 (NLT)**

Here is an amazing acronym that displays a husband's love for his wife. The creator of the acronym wrote, *"Husband is defined as the man who loves me beyond measure."*

He lifts me up when I am down.

Understands me like none other.

Supports my every dream.

Believes in me no matter what.

Accepts me flaws and all.

Nurtures my heart and soul.

Darn ~~near~~ perfect!¹

I love this acronym for **HUSBANDS**. But I must be honest with you. As I read through it, I couldn't help but think about my own needs —that is, the things I want and desire from my wife. What about you? Do you want a wife who lifts you when you are down? A wife who seeks to understand you even when she disagrees? A wife who supports your every dream and puts you before herself? A wife who believes in you no matter what? A wife who accepts you as you are, along with your flaws? A wife who nurtures your heart and soul. A wife is who ~~darn~~ near perfect? How much better would your relationship be if your wife perfected all of these areas of loving you? These are all good things. However, the point is that a loving husband should treat his wife the same way he wants to be treated. Jesus said, "Treat others the same way you want them to treat you." (Luke 6:31)

A husband can do good to his wife by lifting her up when she is down. Have you come home feeling down from having a bad day at work, and needed your wife to encourage you or listen? So it is with your wife! How soothing it is for a wife to have a husband who lifts her when she is down. A husband who is her warm blanket in the chilling snow. A husband who is his wife's sunshine on a cloudy day. A husband who does good to his wife by comforting her. A husband does his good wife good by seeking to understand her. He understands her fears, weaknesses, strengths, concerns, struggles, and imperfections. He understands her and is patient with her, even when he believes she is too emotional about things that, to him, may seem trivial. A husband can do good for his wife by supporting her dreams within reason. In other words, supporting your wife's dreams should not involve pursuing material possessions that will lead to financial struggles down the road. However, a husband can support his wife by recognizing what she wants to accomplish for the marriage, for herself, the children, the household, and so on. She needs emotional support and spiritual support. You can support your wife by praying for her and praying with her. You can encourage her to serve in ministry alongside you. She needs to know that you believe in her talents, gifts, and abilities. She needs to know that she is your most valued possession. You can do your good by accepting her flaws, just as she is. Do you have any flaws? I know I do! I know there are times when I am impatient, prideful, arrogant, stubborn, and selfish. But God still loves me. You and I are sinners in need of God's love, His grace, and His mercy. The same acceptance, the compassion, the same love, the same grace and mercy that God shows towards you is the same loving attitude that you should exhibit towards your wife.

When it comes to being the lender or the borrower, which side of this coin are you on in terms of your relationship with God? Is God the borrower and you the lender? And if God is the Lender, how much has He lent you, and have you paid Him what you owe? Your health and strength, all of your possessions, your wife and children, your job, food, and shelter, your finances, and even the air you breathe are borrowed from God.

What if God measured His blessings, generosity, compassion, and grace toward us based on the one-for-one rule? That's a sobering thought. Yet in His lovingkindness, God has never withheld His provisions. He continues to love us faithfully. So, who are we, then, to withhold love, kindness, and care from our wives? The same love God shows us is the love we are called to show them.

Conclusion

Many husbands struggle to love their wives when they feel they are not receiving enough in return. But this is the world's mindset – "love those who love you." Jesus calls us to a higher standard: to love our wives even when love is not reciprocated (Luke 6:35-37).

Christ Himself is our example. Though He was hated, cursed, and mistreated, He never withdrew His love. Instead, He endured patiently, entrusted Himself to the Father, and gave His life for us (1 Pet. 2:20-24).

Husbands are commanded to love their wives as Christ loved the Church. This means your love cannot be conditional, transactional, or based on what you receive in return. True love is not about self-gratification but about reflecting God's heart. If your motivation for loving your wife is tied only to her response, then your focus is misplaced. Your love must flow from your devotion to God.

Loving your wife is not simply an emotion – it is a choice empowered by the Holy Spirit. Because you belong to Christ, you have been given a new nature and the ability to love with His love. God's love for you is unconditional. And God expects you, as a husband, to reflect that same love toward your wife – especially when it costs you.

And here is the reward: when you love her, expecting nothing in return, you gain something far greater than human recognition. You gain the favor of God—His grace, His mercy, His lovingkindness, and His delight in you.

So, husband, choose to love your wife as Christ loved the Church. Do it not for what you might receive from her, but for the joy of pleasing God. For in loving her unconditionally, you will find yourself loved, blessed, and rewarded by the Lord.

In the next chapter, we will discuss, "Loving your wife when it seems she does not respect your authority."

Reflection Questions

1. In what ways have you been tempted to only love your wife when she shows love in return?

2. What practical steps can you take this week to love your wife without expecting anything back?

3. How might harboring resentment be poisoning your marriage, and what would forgiveness look like instead?

4. How does Christ's example of loving the unlovable encourage you to keep loving your wife faithfully?

Chapter 4

Loving Your Wife When It Seems She Does Not Respect Your Authority

Calling them to Himself, Jesus said, "You know that those who are recognized as rulers of the Gentiles lord it over them; and their great men exercise authority over them. But it is not this way among you, but whoever wishes to become great among you shall be your servant." Mark 10:42-43

Joe and Sarah came for counseling. Sarah professes to be a Christian, while Joe does not. Joe insists he loves his wife because he works hard to provide for her and their children. To him, a man proves his love through provision. He believes that being the breadwinner earns him the right to be the unquestioned authority in the home.

Sarah, however, paints a different picture. She describes Joe as demanding, controlling, and insensitive. She feels overwhelmed by his expectations, ignored when offering her input, and unappreciated for her own hard work both at home and in her full-time job. When Joe reminds her that he is "the man of the house" and therefore deserves respect, she often responds with anger, resentment, and bitterness.

The Problem

Joe's demand for respect is tearing their marriage apart. Instead of leading with love, he rules with force, leaving Sarah feeling devalued and unloved. The home is filled with tension rather than peace, and their relationship resembles that of distant roommates more than husband and wife. But who's to blame for their marriage problems?

The truth is, whenever marriage struggles arise, both spouses contribute to the conflict. Sarah has her own issues to address. Yet as the head of the home, Joe carries a unique responsibility. He is called, by God, to be the loving servant-leader of his home. Yet his misuse of authority—choosing domination instead of servant leadership—is leading their marriage down a destructive path that, if left unchecked, could easily end in divorce.

The World's View of Marital Authority

Across history and cultures, men have often been seen as superior to women, exercising dominance in both society and marriage. This view has led to abusive patterns that persist today.

In some countries, wives are forced into marriage with little say in the matter. In other countries, women must obtain their husband's permission to work. Even worse, many women accept mistreatment as normal, such as in the Democratic Republic of Congo, where a majority of women believe wife-beating is justified under certain circumstances.

In Cambodia, tradition teaches that wives must be soft-spoken caretakers who exist to represent their husbands well in society. Tragically, many women in such contexts see suicide as their only escape from oppression.

Even in the United States, until well into the 20th century, men dominated both home and workplace. Wives were expected to stay home, raise children, and serve their husbands. Older men told younger men not to show weakness, to be aggressive and self-reliant, and to measure their worth by their ability to provide. In some cases, wives would talk to their husbands with their backs turned to them out of submission or out of fear. Moreover, a woman's inheritance automatically went to her husband, and even when women worked, they were typically paid less for the same labor.

Though much has changed – especially with women entering the workforce and contributing significantly to society – traces of the old mindset remain. In many homes today, both husband and wife are educated, employed, and capable. Yet some husbands still cling to the belief that authority belongs exclusively to them. Like Joe in our earlier example, they equate authority with control, forgetting that Scripture calls them to lead in love.

This worldly mindset – whether rooted in domination, tradition, or cultural stereotypes – fails to reflect God's design. Authority in marriage, according to God's design, was never meant to be about superiority or power, but about love, responsibility, and service.

The Dangers of Domination

When a husband demands authority and insists on control, the result can be damaging to his marriage and family. Instead of creating unity, his dominance tears at the foundation of the relationship.

A wife under domination may feel:

- Disrespected – when spoken to rudely or condescendingly.

- Devalued – treated as if her thoughts, opinions, and emotions don't matter.

- Oppressed – burdened and controlled by her husband's expectations.

- Depressed – overwhelmed by sadness or emotional numbness.

- Unloved – unwanted, neglected, and distant from intimacy.

- Unappreciated – feel ignored and taken for granted.

- Hurt – carrying wounds from harsh treatment.

- Lonely – feeling abandoned even while married.

- Afraid – insecure about the marriage's future or fearful of divorce.

- Disconnected – unable to relate due to bitterness and unforgiveness.

- Angry – lashing out, sometimes to protect the children.

The children also suffer under a domineering father:

- They may become fearful, angry, or bitter toward him.

- Sons may grow up imitating their father's harshness with their own wives.

- Daughters may grow up determined never to submit to a husband.

- Adolescents may rebel, carrying resentment well into adulthood.

Domination damages everyone in the household. What looks like strength is actually weakness—a misuse of authority that creates brokenness. In certain instances, a husband's insecurities may drive him to demand authority and control.

Jesus warned His followers against this kind of leadership. "The rulers of the Gentiles lord it over them," He said, "but it is not this way among you" (Mark 10:42-43). God-ordained authority is not about demanding, dictating, or demeaning. It is about serving.

A husband who lords his authority over his wife is not building up his home—he is tearing it down. A dominating husband is a peace-breaker. Like pulling blocks from the foundation of a tower, domination makes collapse inevitable.

Passive Husbands

On the opposite end of the spectrum are husbands who demand respect, seek control, or abuse their authority, and those who avoid conflict altogether by relinquishing their leadership to their wives. These men hand over decision-making to their wives – including managing finances, disciplining children, and setting the direction of the home. They rarely act without their wife's approval, believing that going along with her is the best way to "keep the peace."

At first glance, this may look like harmony. But beneath the surface, it breeds resentment. Why? A passive husband is the opposite of a dominating husband, who is a peace-breaker. A passive husband is usually a peace-faker. A passive husband often suppresses his true feelings out of fear of confrontation. He avoids difficult conversations and chooses silence over honesty. Instead of resolving conflict, he swallows his frustrations until bitterness begins to simmer.

Most passive husbands cannot handle emotional flare-ups. The stress of confrontation feels too heavy, so they retreat. Outwardly, the home appears calm. Inwardly, the husband is weighed down by resentment, disappointment, bitterness, or regret. Over time, he may conclude that his wife no longer respects his leadership, opinions, or ability to provide direction. So he gives up trying.

This dynamic creates disunity and emotional turmoil. The wife grows frustrated with his reluctance to lead. The husband grows angry at what feels like her rejection of him as head of the home. In reality, the house is in disarray, and the relationship suffers.

A passive husband may respond in one of four ways:

1. He learns to live in quiet misery, never addressing the underlying issues.

2. He seeks emotional or physical fulfillment in an adulterous relationship.

3. The marriage ends in divorce.

4. The couple seeks biblical counseling and chooses to pursue God's design for marriage.

The fourth outcome requires the most courage. Change demands confession, forgiveness, repentance, and a renewed commitment to God's order of headship and submission. But with God's help, even a deeply passive husband and an angry wife's marital relationship can be restored.

The Poison of Passivity

If domination destroys marriages through force, passivity poisons them through neglect.

Poison works quietly—entering the body, spreading slowly, and weakening it from within. In the same way, passivity erodes the fabric of marriage. It may look peaceful on the surface, but beneath lies disunity, numbness, and emotional shutdown. Left unchecked, it can lead to a marriage that is legally intact but relationally dead—two people living as roommates instead of one flesh.

A husband, as the god-ordained authority in marriage, does not mean his wife has no voice. She should, and healthy leadership welcomes her input. But when roles are reversed – when the wife takes charge and the husband steps back—the relationship begins to ingest poison. Over time, the wife may lose respect for her husband, doubting his ability to lead or provide security. She may even stop trusting him altogether.

Recovering from years of passivity is difficult, though not impossible. It often requires the Spirit's work and the guidance of biblical counseling. Still, the longer a husband avoids his role, the harder it becomes to reclaim it.

I once knew a man named Robert who often said, "Whatever makes my wife happy makes me happy." At first, it sounded noble. But one day, his wife discovered her "dream home" and insisted they buy it. Though he knew they couldn't afford it, he admitted to me privately, "I don't know how to tell her no." The reason he found it difficult to tell his wife "no" is that his desire to keep the peace outweighed his responsibility to lead.

Robert's attitude mirrors Adam's failure in the Garden of Eden. When Eve reached for the forbidden fruit, Adam was right there. Instead of stepping in, he remained silent. Perhaps he thought, "I don't want to upset her." But by surrendering his God-given role, he fell into sin.

Passivity is not harmless—it is poison. It kills leadership, weakens trust, and corrodes oneness. What begins as an attempt to avoid conflict often ends in greater conflict and disunity.

The Biblical View of Passivity

From the beginning, God established a clear order of authority:

- God over man,

- Man over woman,

- Together entrusted with creation.

God called Adam to lead his wife, yet in the Garden, he failed. When the serpent tempted Eve, Adam stood silently by. Instead of protecting her and obeying God, he allowed her to take the lead and then followed her into sin. This reversal of roles brought chaos, confusion, and ultimately death.

Passivity is not simply weakness; it is disobedience. By refusing to lead, Adam surrendered his God-given responsibility, and humanity has lived with the consequences ever since. Through Eve, Satan set the trap, and Adam took the bait.

Some husbands today fall into the same trap. They want peace at any cost, even if it means sacrificing leadership. Others disguise their passivity under a calm or easygoing demeanor, but beneath the surface lies suppressed anger. Suppressed anger can become "passive-aggression" – a delayed explosion waiting to erupt. Outwardly compliant, inwardly resentful, these men eventually unleash built-up frustration, damaging their wives and families.

At the root of passivity is **the fear of man**. Proverbs 29:25 says, *"The fear of man brings a snare, but he who trusts in the LORD will be exalted."* In Proverbs 29:25, a "snare" is an ancient term that was once commonly used among hunters. A snare is a device hunters use to entrap unsuspecting animals or prey. Being caught in a trap can cause the victim to exhibit erratic behavior. An animal caught in a trap will scream, scratch, claw, bite, shake, and hyperventilate in an attempt to free itself. What does the behavior of an animal caught have to do with the fear of man? The fear of man compels a person to exhibit erratic behavior. Fear of man means being more concerned with pleasing others than obeying God. A passive husband fears his wife's disapproval more than he fears dishonoring God. He avoids conflict, agrees outwardly while disagreeing inwardly, and adopts the motto, "Whatever makes her happy." But this is not leadership – it is a snare.

To break free, a husband must trust God more than he fears his wife. Actual change comes not by lashing out or reclaiming authority with force, but by patiently, gently, and consistently stepping into the role God has assigned, even in the face of opposition. Leadership is not about selfish control—it is about loving responsibility. Besides being a husband who is domineering and passive, the concept of mutual authority in marriage presents another litany of marital problems.

The Question of Mutual Authority

Many new generational couples reject both domination and passivity, instead embracing the idea of *egalitarianism*. Egalitarianism teaches that men and women are completely equal and should share mutual authority in marriage. On the surface, this seems fair and even biblical to some. Husbands and wives are encouraged to make decisions together, share leadership responsibilities, and function as co-heads of the home. Some of which is partially true.

The problem comes when this idea is used to dismiss or distort biblical truths about headship and submission in marriage. Some argue that Scripture supports shared authority, but often this conclusion is based on misinterpretation of Scripture, commonly Ephesians 5:21. The Bible affirms the equal worth and value of men and women, but it also clearly assigns distinct roles.

The Two-Headed Monster – Egalitarianism

In past generations, the husband was almost always viewed as the sole authority in the home. Today, many couples are moving in the opposite direction, embracing *egalitarianism*. Egalitarianism is the belief that a husband and wife share equal authority in every aspect of the marriage—making decisions together, sharing leadership, and exercising mutual submission. On the surface, this seems fair and even appealing, especially in a culture where both spouses often work and contribute financially.

But Does Egalitarianism Align with God's Word?

According to Scripture, equality of worth does not mean sameness of role. Both men and women are made in God's image, equally valuable and deeply loved. Yet God gave husbands and wives distinct functions in the marriage relationship. Egalitarianism, by erasing those distinctions, often produces confusion instead of unity.

Here are some of the problems that arise:

- **Decision-making paralysis** – When husband and wife disagree, who makes the final call?

- **Blame-shifting** – Shared authority can lead to shared irresponsibility when things go wrong.

- **Manipulation by children** – Kids quickly learn to exploit divided leadership, playing one parent against the other.

- **Stunted growth** – Instead of thriving, the marriage becomes stagnant, lacking clarity and direction.

Communal authority may sound like a partnership, but in practice, it often creates division. Just as two captains cannot steer one ship, a marriage cannot flourish to its fullest potential with two heads. God's design for the hierarchy of marriage is clear: Christ is the head of every man, man is the head of woman, and

God is the head of Christ (1 Corinthians 11:3). Authority in marriage, rightly exercised, is meant to reflect that divine order—not compete with it.

So the question remains: *What do you do when it seems your wife does not respect your authority?*

- The dominating husband demands respect and uses control.

- The passive husband relinquishes leadership and avoids conflict.

- The egalitarian husband embraces shared authority and sees both he and his wife as co-heads.

The truth is, none of these approaches fully reflects God's design. Authority in marriage must be defined not by cultural trends or personal preference, but by Scripture itself. Before we can understand how to love our wives when respect is lacking, we must first ask: **What is biblical authority, and what does it look like in practice?**

The Biblical View of Marital Authority

The godly husband exercises his godly-ordained authority by leading and loving his wife as Christ the church.

The apostle Paul wrote, *"Be imitators of me, just as I also am of Christ... I want you to understand that Christ is the head of every man, and the man is the head of a woman, and God is the head of Christ."* (1 Corinthians 11:1-3 NASB)

This passage affirms both equality and distinction. Men and women are equal in value before God, yet different in role. From creation, God established a divine order:

1. Adam was formed first from the dust (Gen. 2:7).

2. Adam was given authority to name the animals (Gen. 2:19).

3. Eve was created from Adam's rib as his helper (Gen. 2:22–23).

4. Adam named her "woman," and later "Eve" (Gen. 3:20).

These details show that while man and woman are equal in worth, God gave man a distinct leadership role. This biblical order of hierarchy is not cultural but built into creation itself.

The New Testament deepens this truth:

- *"For the husband is the head of the wife, as Christ also is the head of the church, He Himself being the Savior of the body"* (Ephesians 5:23 NASB).

- The Greek word for "head" (κεφαλή, *kephalē*) conveys authority and position, which is given by one who is superior.

- Christ models this headship as a **servant-leader** – one who sacrifices for the good of others (Matthew 20:26-28; John 13:13-17).

Biblical authority, then, is not about domination or passivity. Nor is it about communal equality that erases roles. It is about servant leadership: the husband leading his wife as Christ leads the church – with humility, sacrifice, and love.

A husband's authority is not a license to rule harshly, nor is his leadership earned by income, or deserved by education, or skill. It is God-given, rooted in creation, and patterned after Christ. And because Christ's authority is exercised in service, so must a husband's be.

So What?

Biblically, headship is not earned through masculinity, education, or income. Authority in marriage is granted by God's design. The real question is not *whether* a husband has authority, but *how* he chooses to exercise it.

The call is clear: a husband must not demand respect or shrink into passivity. Instead, he is to lead through love. This means:

- **Serving** his wife before himself.

- **Sacrificing** for her needs.

- **Honoring** her as a precious jewel and handling her with care as fine china that is easily broken.

- **Building** her up with encouragement rather than tearing her down.

- **Caring** for her as a shepherd tenderly carries his sheep.

- **Guiding** her as a priest intercedes for those in his care.

True headship mirrors Christ's relationship with the church. Jesus did not coerce His bride—He loved her, served her, and gave Himself up for her. In the same way, a husband's authority must be marked by grace, patience, and sacrificial love.

Authority, rightly understood, is not about power but about responsibility. It is a calling to reflect Christ by laying down one's life for his wife.

Prohibitions to Authority

Jesus warned His disciples:

> *"You know that those who are recognized as rulers of the Gentiles lord it over them, and their great men exercise authority over them. But it is not this way among you; but whoever wishes to become great among you shall be your servant."* (Mark 10:42-43)

Marital leadership is not about being a commander-in-chief. It is not harsh, insensitive, or arrogant. Biblical authority is not something to be demanded, fought for, or proven in arguments. When a husband insists on his authority through quarrels and ultimatums, he undermines the very authority he seeks to defend.

Instead, a husband must exercise leadership the way Christ did—through patience, gentleness, and service. What should you do when it seems your wife does not respect your authority? You resist the urge to demand it and instead:

- **Show kindness** through practical acts of love.

- **Teach gently**, admonishing her when necessary with care and humility.

- **Practice patience**, bearing with her weaknesses and offenses.

- **Encourage and console**, especially when she feels discouraged.

- **Support her**, walking with her in struggles and temptations.

You must always exercise authority with tenderness. Your wife is the "weaker vessel" (1 Peter 3:7), not in value but in design. She is to be handled like fine crystal—treasured and protected, never crushed.

By leading with gentleness rather than force, a husband demonstrates true biblical authority: not lording it over his wife, but loving her as Christ loves the church.

Illustration

If you've ever watched *Hell's Kitchen*, you've seen how an executive chef can demand perfection while berating and belittling his cooks. The show portrays executive chef Gordon Ramsay as harsh, rude, and insensitive – all in the name of authority and food. While many assume this is just entertainment, I can tell you from my years as a professional chef: such behavior is all too common in real kitchens.

I trained under chefs who raged, shouted, and verbally abused their teams. Though I learned valuable lessons about excellence, I also decided I would lead differently when I became an executive chef. I believed in pursuing perfection, but without cruelty.

One day, an employee told me, "Respect must be earned." I replied, perhaps a bit bluntly, "I don't have to respect you, but you must respect me." What I meant was, as their superior, I bore responsibility for the kitchen's success, and with responsibility comes authority. Yet, I chose to exercise that authority differently from Chef Ramsay.

Instead of ruling by fear, I practiced servant leadership. I invested in my employees—teaching them skills, encouraging them through struggles, and even serving them meals during team-building events. I wanted them to grow, not just perform. As a result, they respected me not because I demanded it, but because they knew I cared.

This principle applies even more in marriage. A husband's authority is not to be wielded like a tyrannical chef, barking orders. It is to be lived out like Christ, who *"did not come to be served, but to serve"* (Matthew 20:28). Servant leadership doesn't diminish authority—it strengthens it.

When you love your wife sacrificially, she responds with respect, not because you force it, but because she knows you value her. Just as my kitchen employees flourished under servant leadership, so too can a marriage thrive when a husband leads with humility and love.

Why Should You Love Your Wife If She Does Not Respect Your Authority?

What if Jesus asked you the same question: *"Why should I love you when you do not always respect My authority?"*

The truth is, every husband falls short. At times, you fail to honor God's authority, yet He continues to love you. He is patient, gracious, and merciful—even when you are stubborn, selfish, or disobedient. His love is not based on your performance but on His character.

Paul reminds us:

> *"But God demonstrates His own love toward us, in that while we were yet sinners, Christ died for us."* (Romans 5:8)

Jesus loved you when you were at your worst. He sacrificed for you, not because you deserved it, but because it glorified the Father. That same love is the model for how you are to love your wife.

Paul also wrote:

"So husbands ought also to love their own wives as their own bodies. He who loves his own wife loves himself; for no one ever hated his own flesh, but nourishes and cherishes it, just as Christ also does the church." (Ephesians 5:28-29)

When you get married, you become one flesh with your wife. Loving her is, in reality, loving yourself. When she hurts, you hurt. When she thrives, you thrive. To neglect her is to neglect yourself.

Marriage is not like employment—you cannot simply "terminate" your wife when she disappoints you. She is part of you. God calls you to a lifetime of faithfulness, even when she struggles to respect your authority.

In the end, the reason you love your wife – even when respect feels absent—is not because she has earned it, but because Christ loved the church in this way. He calls you to love her sacrificially, unconditionally, and faithfully, for this is how God is glorified in marriage.

Conclusion

When it seems your wife does not respect your authority, your calling is not to demand, retreat, or compromise God's design. Your calling is to love.

Love that is rooted not in feelings but in obedience to God.

Love that is expressed not in domination or silence, but in service and sacrifice.

Love that reflects Christ's love for His bride, the church.

To love this way means choosing to:

- Lead with humility, not pride.

- Serve with patience, not harshness.

- Build up with encouragement, not criticism.

- Sacrifice for her good, not your comfort.

Why should you love your wife when she does not seem to respect you? Because this is precisely how Christ loved you.

Marriage is not sustained by demands for respect or by avoiding conflict. It is strengthened when a husband chooses to reflect Christ – laying down his life, leading with grace, and loving with faithfulness.

God has called you to nothing less.

In the next chapter, we will discuss, "Loving your wife when she has offended you."

Reflection Questions

1. In what ways do you see tendencies of domination or passivity in your own marriage? How have they affected your relationship with your wife?

2. How does Christ's model of servant leadership challenge the way you currently exercise authority in your home?

3. When was the last time you loved your wife sacrificially, not because of her response, but out of obedience to God? What did that look like?

4. What practical steps can you take this week to reflect Christ's love—through service, encouragement, patience, or sacrifice—in your relationship with your wife?

Chapter 5

Loving Your Wife When She Has Offended You

The 2008 Tyler Perry film *The Family That Preys* illustrates the pain of offense in marriage. Chris (Rockmond Dunbar) and Andrea (Sanaa Lathan) are a working-class couple. Chris, recently unemployed, struggles to find work, while Andrea thrives in her oil company career and has just been promoted to a six-figure salary.

Her success brings new benefits: luxury purchases, furniture, clothes, and even a company car. But Andrea makes these decisions without consulting Chris. One day, while Andrea was at work, Chris began walking around the house making observations of the expensive purchases that Andrea had accumulated over the last several months, and he became curious about where all of her money was coming from. That evening, when Andrea arrived home, Chris had a few questions for her about her spending. When she entered the door, he calmly asked,

"I am just curious where all this money they are using to make all of these purchases is coming from?" Her response was not what Chris expected.

She exploded: "Who are you to question me about my money, Chris? The money I work hard for!"

When Chris pressed further, she sucker-punched him with her words by comparing Chris unfavorably to her boss:

"He's caring, educated, and successful—everything you're not. So don't you dare question me about my money!"

Andrea, seemingly relieved to voice her frustrations, walks away without remorse. Her words pierce Chris's heart. Wounded and humiliated, he sits speechless, eyes filled with tears. Chris withdraws in silence, refusing to speak to her for weeks.

The Problem

Here is a man who is broken by his wife's cutting words. Andrea reminded him of his unemployment, insulted his manhood, and elevated another man above him. For any husband, few wounds cut more deeply than being demeaned by his wife and being compared unfavorably to another man.

If Andrea were your wife, how would you have responded? Explosive anger? Silent withdrawal?

Most husbands know this pain. Maybe your wife has criticized more than encouraged, highlighted your faults more than your strengths, or left you feeling unappreciated and inadequate. You are not alone.

But here's the challenge: even when your wife offends you, God still calls you to love her. Offense does not release you from the biblical command: *"Husbands, love your wives, just as Christ also loved the church and gave Himself up for her..."* (Ephesians 5:25)

Your wife's words may stem from sin—or they may express legitimate concerns poorly. Either way, your response must reflect Christ. Any offense that your wife commits against you is not an excuse to retaliate; it is an opportunity to love, admonish with gentle correction, nourish, and cherish her as Christ does the church. But to Judge and condemn her is not the Christlike response.

Do Not Judge Your Wife

"Do not judge so that you will not be judged. For in the way you judge, you will be judged; and by your standard of measure, it will be measured to you. Why do you look at the speck that is in your brother's eye, but do not notice the log that is in your own eye? ... First take the log out of your own eye, and then you will see clearly to take the speck out of your brother's eye." (Matthew 7:1-5)

What does it mean to judge?

Christians have long debated whether judging others is ever appropriate. Some argue that judging is necessary to hold people accountable, while others insist judgment belongs only to God. Scripture shows both perspectives:

- "Do not judge according to appearance, but judge with righteous judgment." (John 7:24)

- "If anyone hears My sayings and does not keep them, I do not judge him..." (John 12:47)

- "Do you not know that the saints will judge the world?" (1 Corinthians 6:2)

- "For what have I to do with judging outsiders? Do you not judge those who are within the church?" (1 Corinthians 5:12)

So which is right? The key lies in understanding two kinds of judgment:

- **Righteous judgment** aligns with God's Word, identifying right and wrong without arrogance. It seeks restoration, not destruction.

- **Human judgment** presumes to know motives and then seeks to condemn and punish the offender. Human judgment flows from pride and anger, not truth and love.

When Jesus warns in Matthew 7:1, He speaks against human judgment. Only God fully knows the heart (Jeremiah 17:9–10). Our role is not to condemn but to discern rightly and respond with humility.

So, should you judge your wife when she offends you? Yes, but only by declaring sinful behavior as sin, in line with Scripture. For example, if she disrespects you or undermines your God-given role, you may rightly call it wrong. But the danger comes when righteous judgment slides into human judgment – when correction is laced with anger, resentment, and bitterness.

If you label your wife "useless" in your heart, even if the words never leave your lips, you have crossed into sinful judgment. Jesus warns against this. Your calling is not to judge but to correct gently, in love and humility, and seek to restore her and your relationship. But to exercise human judgment on your wife is to condemn her.

Do Not Condemn Your Wife

Jesus warns: *Do not judge so that you will not be judged. For in the way you judge, you will be judged; and by your standard of measure, it will be measured to you.* (Matthew 7:1-2)

Condemnation goes beyond identifying sin – it declares someone guilty and deserving of punishment. In a courtroom, a judge weighs evidence, delivers a verdict, and issues a sentence. Condemnation in marriage works the same way: you set yourself up as judge, jury, and executioner over your wife.

James cautions:

> *"Do not speak against one another, brethren. He who speaks against a brother or judges his brother speaks against the law... There is only one Lawgiver and Judge, the One who is able to save*

and to destroy; but who are you who judge your neighbor?(James 4:11-12)

To "speak against" someone means to slander—to belittle, insult, or defame. This includes gossip, criticism, angry outbursts, cruel words, or profanity. When you condemn your wife with such speech, you not only wound her but also set yourself against God's law.

You may ask, *But shouldn't I confront my wife's sin?* Yes, you should (Matthew 18:15; Galatians 6:1). But confrontation must be loving, not condemning. To lash out with slander or harsh words is to elevate yourself above God, as if you were the lawgiver. Only God has the authority to condemn.

Furthermore, when you condemn your wife, you harm the marriage, dishonor God, and condemn yourself. However, if you confront her with humility and grace, you honor God and open the door for healing. God will judge you in the same way that you judge your wife.

In the Way You Judge, You Will Be Judged

Jesus adds weight to His warning: *For in the way you judge, you will be judged; and by your standard of measure, it will be measured to you.* (Matthew 7:2)

We know the sayings: *What goes around comes around,* and *you reap what you sow.* These truths reflect Jesus' teaching. The way you treat others – especially your wife – sets the standard by which God will measure you.

If you condemn your wife with harshness, you invite God's discipline. Avoidance, cold silence, belittling, slander, neglect, withholding intimacy, angry outbursts, or even bitterness are all forms of condemnation. If you persist in them, God may allow you to experience distance in prayer, strained relationships, or withheld blessings.

Luke records it this way: *Do not judge, and you will not be judged; and do not condemn, and you will not be condemned; pardon, and you will be pardoned* (Luke 6:37).

The principle is simple: you get what you give. If you extend grace, you will receive grace. If you forgive, you will be forgiven. But if you condemn, you will be condemned.

Yes, your wife may have offended you. But consider this: have you not offended God far more? And how did He respond? With patience, mercy, and forgiveness. Should you not do the same for your wife? Moreover, you should avoid always pointing out her faults without seeing your own.

Avoid the One-Way Mirror Syndrome

Jesus continues: "Why do you look at the speck that is in your brother's eye, but do not notice the log that is in your own eye? ... First take the log out of your own eye, and then you will see clearly to take the speck out of your brother's eye." (Matthew 7:3-5)

Police often use a one-way mirror during lineups. Observers can see suspects, but the suspects cannot see them. In marriage, the "one-way mirror syndrome" occurs when you magnify your wife's faults while ignoring your own. You see her "speck" but remain blind to the "log" in your eye.

Here is another illustration called *The Dirty Window*

Mark was frustrated with his wife, Lisa. Every morning, as he sat at the kitchen table sipping coffee, he noticed the neighbor's laundry hanging on the clothesline. "Look at that," he muttered. "She never washes them properly—those sheets are always so dingy."

For weeks, Mark peered through the window and grumbled about the neighbor's dirty sheets. Lisa mostly stayed quiet, though she grew weary of his constant criticism. One Saturday, he came to the table ready to complain again, but this time he stopped short. The sheets looked bright and clean.

"Finally," he said, "Ah, the neighbor learned how to wash!"

Lisa set a plate in front of him and replied gently, "No, Mark. I got up early and washed our kitchen window."

The problem wasn't the neighbor's laundry – it was the dirt on his own glass.

In the same way, it's easy for a husband to magnify his wife's faults while overlooking his own. The speck in her life looks huge because the "log" in his own life clouds his vision. True clarity – and true healing – only comes when he cleans his own window first.

It's always easier to point out our wives' sins than to face our own. But reconciliation, unity, and healing cannot come until both husband and wife confess their failures. And as the leader, it must start with you.

If you only focus on your wife's offense, you will stay stuck in pride, anger, and defensiveness. But if you examine yourself first, you will lead the way toward humility and restoration.

Examine Yourself First

Jesus calls the one who judges without self-examination a hypocrite: "You hypocrite, first take the log out of your own eye, and then you will see clearly to take the speck out of your brother's eye." Matthew 7:5

When does a husband become a hypocrite? A hypocrite pretends to be righteous while ignoring his own sin. He points out his wife's faults but overlooks his own failures as a husband. Authentic leadership begins with honest self-examination.

- David prayed: "Search me, O God, and know my heart; Try me and know my anxious thoughts." Psalm 139:23

- Jeremiah urged: "Let us examine and probe our ways and let us return to the LORD." Lamentations 3:40

- Paul wrote: "Test yourselves to see if you are in the faith; examine yourselves!" 2 Corinthians 13:5

Before addressing your wife's offense, you must ask:

1. Am I loving her sacrificially as Christ loved the church (Ephesians 5:25-28)?

2. Am I living with her in understanding, honoring her as fragile and precious (1 Peter 3:7)?

3. Am I leading with humility, valuing her thoughts and needs (1 Timothy 5:8)?

Often, when you examine yourself honestly, you discover the "log" of pride, selfishness, or neglect is far greater than the "speck" you see in her. Self-examination humbles you and prepares you to approach her with grace instead of condemnation. But you must address your log first.

Take the Log Out of Your Eye

When Andrea lashed out at Chris in *The Family That Preys*, her words were harsh and wounding. Yet before judging her, Chris needed to examine himself. Had he, as a husband, been loving her sacrificially and leading with understanding?

Paul writes: "Husbands, love your wives, just as Christ also loved the church and gave Himself up for her..." Ephesians 5:25 (NASB)

Scripture also says:

> "You husbands in the same way, live with your wives in an understanding way, as with someone weaker, since she is a woman; and show her honor as a fellow heir of the grace of life, so that your prayers will not be hindered." (1 Peter 3:7)

Chris's failures – unemployment, neglect, poor leadership – did not excuse Andrea's outburst, but they did contribute to the conflict. Often, a wife's offense is magnified by a husband's failure to love, protect, and lead well.

Taking the log out of your eye means owning your part first. It means confessing where you have failed before addressing her faults. This is not weakness – it is spiritual leadership. By humbling yourself, you create space for healing and reconciliation. Once you remove the log from your eye, then you will be able to address the speck in her eye.

See Clearly to Remove the Speck

Jesus says, "First take the log out of your own eye, and then you will see clearly to take the speck out of your brother's eye." Matthew 7:5

Clarity comes through humility. Until you face your own sin, your vision will be clouded by pride, anger, or self-righteousness. You will speak from woundedness rather than wisdom. But when you confess your failures first, your heart softens, and you can approach your wife with grace instead of judgment.

Paul echoes this: *Brethren, even if anyone is caught in any trespass, you who are spiritual, restore such a one in a spirit of gentleness; each one looking to yourself, so that you too will not be tempted.* Galatians 6:1

The word *restore* pictures a doctor carefully setting a broken bone or a fisherman mending torn nets. Both require patience, precision, and gentleness. In the same way, confronting your wife's offense must be done not with a hammer, but with healing hands.

Seeing clearly means you check your motives:

- Am I addressing this to restore her, or to win the argument?

- Am I correcting her to build unity, or to prove I'm right?

- Am I motivated by love for her, or frustration with her?

If the answer is anything but love, you are not ready. Step back, examine your heart, pray, and seek the Spirit's help before you speak.

When you approach your wife with humility, she is far more likely to listen. Even if she resists at first, your gentleness will plant seeds of reconciliation. Remember: your goal is not to defeat your wife – it is to win her heart. Love her unconditionally.

Love Your Wife Even When Offended

Paul writes: "Husbands, love your wives, just as Christ also loved the church and gave Himself up for her..." Ephesians 5:25

The command to love your wife does not come with conditions. It does not say, *"Love her when she respects you,"* or *Love her when she treats you kindly.* It simply says, *Love your wives of Christ loved the Church.*

Offense does not excuse you from obedience. In fact, moments of offense test whether your love is rooted in Christ or in convenience. When your wife wounds you with words or actions, you stand at a crossroads of *Should I:*

- React in the flesh – withdraw, retaliate, or condemn.

- Respond in the Spirit – forgive, pursue, and love.

Christ loved you when you were at your worst – rebellious, selfish, and undeserving. He laid down His life for you, not because you earned it, but because it glorified the Father. That is the model for a husband's love.

To love your wife when she has offended you means:

- Refusing to replay her words over and over in your mind.

- Choosing forgiveness instead of bitterness.

- Speaking gently when you'd rather lash out.

- Seeking reconciliation rather than victory.

- Praying for her instead of judging her.

Love is not blind to offense – it sees it clearly, but chooses to cover it with grace. Peter reminds us: *Above all, keep fervent in your love for one another, because love covers a multitude of sins.* 1 Peter 4:8

When you love your wife even in offense, you reflect the heart of Christ, who covered your sins with His blood.

Do Not Be Bitter Against Your Wife

Paul commands: *Husbands, love your wives and do not be embittered against them."* Colossians 3:19

Bitterness begins small—a harsh word, a cold shoulder, a repeated offense. Left unchecked, it takes root in the heart, growing into resentment and hostility. A bitter husband stores up offenses, replaying them until his love is poisoned.

Bitterness shows itself in many ways:

- Harsh or sarcastic words.

- Silent withdrawal and emotional distance.

- Holding grudges instead of forgiving.

- Withdrawing affection, intimacy, or kindness.

- Treating your wife more like an enemy than a partner.

The danger of bitterness is that it does not stay hidden. It subtly spills into every part of the marriage – your communication, intimacy, parenting, even your prayers. Paul warns that bitterness grieves the Holy Spirit (Ephesians 4:30–31).

The cure for bitterness is forgiveness. Forgiveness does not excuse the offense, but it releases the debt. It frees both you and your wife from the chains of resentment. Paul instructs:

"Let all bitterness and wrath and anger and clamor and slander be put away from you, along with all malice. Be kind to one another, tender-hearted, forgiving each other, just as God in Christ also has forgiven you." (Ephesians 4:31–32)

When you choose forgiveness over bitterness, you reflect Christ, who forgave you an immeasurable debt. A forgiving husband creates space for healing, intimacy, and peace in the home. But how often should you forgive your wife, especially if she commits the same offense?

Peter once asked Jesus: "Lord, how often shall my brother sin against me and I forgive him? Up to seven times?" Jesus said to him, "I do not say to you, up to seven times, but up to seventy times seven." Matthew 18:21-22

Forgiveness is not about keeping score. Jesus' answer makes clear – if you are counting wrongs, you are not truly forgiving. Forgiveness must be continual, just as God continually forgives you.

Paul echoes this truth: "Be kind to one another, tender-hearted, forgiving each other, just as God in Christ also has forgiven you." Ephesians 4:32

There will be occasions when your wife will offend you deeply. But the gospel leaves no room for bitterness or grudges. If Christ forgave you – entirely, freely, and undeservedly – then you must extend the same grace to her.

Forgiveness does not mean you ignore sin. It means you release the right to punish. It means you confront your wife with love, not condemnation. It means you choose reconciliation over revenge.

To forgive your wife is to reflect Christ Himself. It is an act of obedience, a step of faith, and a testimony to the power of the gospel at work in your marriage. So forgiveness is a Christ-like response to an offense.

Conclusion

Marriage is not free from offense. At times, your wife will wound you with her words or actions. Yet an offense is not a license for retaliation, withdrawal, or bitterness. It is an opportunity to reflect Christ.

Jesus loved you when you were unlovable, forgave you when you were guilty, and bore your offenses on the cross. In the same way, you are called to love, forgive, and pursue your wife – even when she offends you.

Your response to offenses reveals the source of your love. If your love for your wife depends on her behavior, it will crumble under disappointment. But if your love flows from Christ, it will endure, heal, and strengthen your marriage.

To love your wife when offended is to follow in the footsteps of Christ, who gave Himself up for His bride. This is not weakness – it is true strength, rooted in obedience to God and empowered by His Spirit.

In the next chapter, we will discuss, "Loving your wife when she seems like an enemy."

Reflection Questions

1. When your wife last offended you, how did you respond—reacting in the flesh or responding in the Spirit? How was your response pleasing to God?

2. What "logs" in your own life do you need to examine before addressing the "specks" in your wife's eye?

3. Where has bitterness taken root in your heart, and what steps can you take, from this chapter, to replace it with forgiveness?

4. How can you practically reflect Christ's love this week when an offense arises in your marriage?

Chapter 6
Loving Your Wife When She Seems Like an Enemy

In 1989, a dark comedy called *The War of the Roses* hit theaters, starring Michael Douglas and Kathleen Turner as Oliver and Barbara Rose. At first glance, they seemed to have a picture-perfect marriage: Oliver was a successful attorney, and Barbara was the devoted wife who supported him. Yet, over time, cracks appeared. Oliver became critical, blaming Barbara for spoiling their children, while remaining blind to his own self-centered, controlling behavior. Barbara, meanwhile, grew increasingly resentful until love turned into hostility.

After twenty years together, they became bitter enemies under the same roof. Divorce proceedings escalated into a vicious war — not only over possessions but over pride and control. Their attacks turned verbal, then destructive, even dangerous. They declare war against one another. They begin verbally attacking and humiliating each other in every way possible, even in front of friends and potential business clients. Both start destroying the house furnishings: the stove, furniture, Staffordshire ornaments, and dishware. In addition, Oliver accidentally runs over Barbara's cat in the driveway. When Barbara finds out, she retaliates by trapping Oliver inside his private sauna, where he nearly succumbs to heatstroke and dehydration.

At the movie's end, Oliver and Barbara's quarrel has culminated in the two of them hanging dangerously from the insecure chandelier. The wire eventually fails, sending Oliver, Barbara, and the chandelier crashing violently to the floor. In the film's tragic climax, they both fall to their deaths, clinging to a chandelier that could not hold them.

What a heartbreaking ending. A marriage that began with love and promise ended in mutual destruction. Oliver and Barbara once shared everything — home, children, and years of life together — yet they chose rivalry over reconciliation.

When Your Wife Feels Like the Enemy

Are there times when your wife seems more like your adversary than your partner? . She knows you better than anyone else – your strengths, your weaknesses, and your faults. Like most husbands, you may want your wife to affirm you. But she can call you out when you're wrong, hold you accountable when you fall short, and even express anger when she feels hurt. At times, this can feel like disrespect or rejection.

Maybe you've experienced nights where you retreat to the sofa while she stays in the bedroom. Conversations shrink to bare necessities. Intimacy fades. Acts of kindness, meals, or simple favors disappear. You begin to feel like you're on the opposing side of a battle. Perhaps you try breaking the ice with love, but she doesn't respond. You offer help, but it goes unnoticed. You give of yourself, yet nothing is given back. Frustration builds until you begin to wonder if separation – emotional or even physical – is the only way forward.

The truth is that some couples live "separate" lives under the same roof. Emotional, mental, physical, and spiritual distance can grow until the home feels divided.

So how do you respond when your wife feels like your enemy? The Bible gives a clear command:

"Husbands, love your wives and do not be embittered against them." (Colossians 3:19)

Bitterness is often the hidden enemy of love. It tempts you to withdraw, become defensive, shift blame, or bury yourself in work to avoid her. Some husbands even seek comfort in the arms of another woman. But these reactions do not solve the problem – they only deepen the divide.

Love Your Wife as Your Neighbor

So how can you love your wife when she feels like your enemy? Is there hope for a marriage that seems broken? The answer is yes – there is always hope. With God's help, love can be restored, reconciliation can happen, and what feels lost can be renewed. The Scriptures provide us with practical steps for overcoming the challenge of loving our wives when they seem like our enemies:

You must love your neighbor.

But who is your neighbor? Jesus answered this question clearly:

> "'You shall love the Lord your God with all your heart, and with all your soul, and with all your mind.' This is the great and foremost commandment. The second is like it: 'You shall love your neighbor as yourself." (Matthew 22:37–39)

To love God is to devote every part of who you are – your thoughts, emotions, words, choices, and will – to Him. But Jesus makes it clear that our love for God is revealed in how we love others. If you want to measure your love for God, look at how you treat your neighbor.

Consider the encounter between Jesus and a lawyer recorded in Luke 10. This lawyer, an expert in Mosaic Law, asked Jesus, "Teacher, what shall I do to inherit eternal life?" Jesus responded with a question of His own: "What does the Law say?" The lawyer summarized Scripture well, quoting:

"'You shall love the Lord your God with all your heart, and with all your soul, and with all your strength, and with all your mind; and your neighbor as yourself.'" (Luke 10:27)

Jesus commended his answer, but the lawyer pressed further: *And who is my neighbor?* Like many Jews of that time, he believed "neighbor" referred only to fellow Israelites or close companions. The teachers of the Law even went so far as to suggest the opposite of a "neighbor" is an "enemy," and therefore enemies were to be hated.

But Jesus corrected this misunderstanding through the parable of the Good Samaritan (Luke 10:30–37). In this story, Jesus showed that a neighbor is anyone near us, even someone we might see as an enemy. True love extends beyond social circles, beyond convenience, and beyond comfort.

So, who is your closest neighbor?

Jesus tells us how are our neighbors. He said,

"We love because He first loved us. If anyone says, 'I love God,' and hates his brother, he is a liar; for he who does not love his brother whom he has seen cannot love God whom he has not seen. And this commandment we have from Him: whoever loves God must also love his brother." (1 John 4:19-21)

In John 4:19, the noun "brother" refers broadly to fellow believers, but in the most personal sense, your closest neighbor is your wife. If she is in Christ, she is not only your wife but also your sister in the Lord. Marital relations may sometimes be challenging, and yet it is God's primary tool to refine you. Through marital conflict, God often exposes imperfections and uses them to purify both husband and wife.

Your love for God is evidenced by how you love your wife.

Love Your Wife Even When She Opposes You

Jesus sets the standard in Luke 6:27-28 when he said, "But I say to you who hear, love your enemies, do good to those who hate you, bless those who curse you, pray for those who mistreat you."

In Luke 6:27-28, Jesus gives four imperatives, or commands, and they are to *love, do good, bless*, and *pray*. "To Good" can also translated "kindness." These are God's commands for how to respond when faced with opposition. Where there is hatred, respond with love. Where there is cursing, respond with blessing. Where there is mistreatment, respond with prayer.

These Christlike responses are not natural to us – they are supernatural. Jesus calls us to relate to those who oppose us in the exact opposite way they relate to us. And for a husband, that means even if your wife feels like an adversary, you must still love her.

But what does it mean for a wife to feel like an enemy? An enemy is someone who opposes or resists you. Sometimes, even within marriage, those patterns can appear.

An enemy may:

- Speak negatively or destructively about you

- Expose your flaws to others

- Criticize you often

- Show contempt through words, tone, or body language

- Use your past failures against you

- Highlight your weaknesses while ignoring your strengths

- Hold onto anger overnight

- Use hurtful words in arguments

- Keep a record of wrongs

- Accuse you falsely

- Question your motives unfairly

- Twist your words to use against you

- Condemn you for the very things they are guilty of doing themselves

- Magnify your faults while minimizing their own

When your wife exhibits these kinds of behaviors, it can feel like she has become your opponent. Yet Jesus commands us to love even in this context – with agape love, a love of choice, not mere feelings. This kind of love is undeserved, unearned, and unconditional.

Love Your Wife with Acts of Goodness

How do you put love into practice when your wife feels like your enemy? Scripture points us to goodness:

- Exodus 23:4 says, "If you meet your enemy's ox or his donkey wandering away, you shall surely return it to him."

- Solomon wrote, "If your enemy is hungry, give him bread to eat, and if he is thirsty, give him water to drink." (Proverbs 25:21)

We have already discussed what it means to "do good" in chapter 3. Here, let's consider "doing good" as expressions of grace. Acts of goodness mean meeting needs, doing what is right, and seeking the other person's good – even when they don't deserve it. For a husband, that means looking for practical ways to love your wife when tension is high.

What does goodness toward your wife look like?

- Giving her what rightfully belongs to her – your time, attention, and commitment.

- Surprising her with kindness when she least expects it.

- Noticing her needs and meeting them without expecting anything in return.

- Encouraging her when she feels weary or discouraged.

- Refusing to retaliate, even when you feel hurt.

- Working to win her heart by doing good consistently.

- Overcoming wrongs with goodness instead of escalating conflict.

Goodness does not mean ignoring problems, but it does mean choosing to respond in a way that honors Christ. In marriage, goodness, is akin to grace, and is often the bridge that leads back to connection.

So how do you love your wife when she seems like your enemy? Love her as your closest neighbor by responding with acts of goodness. But blessing your wife is also an expression of love.

Love Your Wife by Blessing Her

Jesus repeated the command in Luke 6:27-28, "But I say to you who hear, love your enemies, do good to those who hate you, bless those who curse you, pray for those who mistreat you."

To "bless" means to speak well of, to show favor, and to wish good upon another. The opposite is to "curse" – to hurl insults, speak evil of, or use words that wound. Cursing doesn't always mean profanity; it can also be harsh criticism, name-calling, or words designed to cut deep.

At times, your wife may speak words that hurt you or perform actions that feel like a curse. Yet Jesus calls you to respond in the opposite spirit: with a blessing. Instead of returning insult for insult, you are to give her words of life.

Here are ways you can bless your wife:

- Recognize her strengths – highlight her accomplishments, talents, and wise decisions.

- Express appreciation for qualities you admire, such as her nurturing spirit, her care for the children, or her ability to manage the home.

- Affirm her publicly – speak well of her in front of others, acknowledging her concern for people, her spiritual gifts, or her stewardship of finances.

- Show tangible appreciation – through flowers, a handwritten note, a thoughtful gift, or quality time together.

- Use gentle correction when she has wronged you – sharing your heart with humility rather than condemning her.

Blessing your wife doesn't mean ignoring her hurtful words or pretending everything is fine. It means choosing to build her up instead of tearing her down.

Point: If your wife curses you, your calling is to bless her in return.

Love Your Wife by Praying for Her

Prayer is one of the most powerful expressions of love. Scripture urges us to "pray without ceasing" and assures us that "the effective prayer of a righteous man can accomplish much" (James 5:16; 1 Thess. 5:17).

But in Luke 6:28, Jesus emphasizes a specific kind of prayer. He said, "Pray for those who mistreat you."

This is intercessory prayer, which means to pray on behalf of another, or to bring the needs of another before God, even when that person has hurt you. It's not easy to pray for someone who feels like an adversary, but prayer invites God's power into the relationship and begins to soften hearts, both yours and hers.

Scripture gives us examples:

- Paul prayed that believers would be "filled with the knowledge of His will in all spiritual wisdom" (Col. 1:9-12).

- James urged Christians to pray for one another so that healing could take place (James 5:16).

- Jesus prayed for His enemies on the cross: "Father, forgive them, for they do not know what they are doing" (Luke 23:34).

- Stephen, while being stoned, cried out, "Lord, do not hold this sin against them!" (Acts 7:60).

If these faithful leaders could pray for those actively persecuting them, surely husbands can pray for their wives in moments of conflict.

So, has your wife ever mistreated you? Then your response must be prayer. Intercede for her – asking God for her protection, healing, restoration, and spiritual growth. Pray that she would experience God's grace, forgiveness, and renewal. And don't forget to pray for yourself as well, that God would expose your own sin, soften your heart, and help you seek forgiveness when needed.

Point: If it feels as though your wife has mistreated you, your responsibility is clear – pray for her.

Christ is Our Example.

Christ Himself modeled how to love in the face of opposition. The religious leaders of His day – the scribes, Pharisees, and teachers of the Law – should have been His closest neighbors, yet they were often His fiercest enemies. They rejected Him, ridiculed Him, falsely accused Him, spat on Him, and eventually nailed Him to the cross.

And yet, Jesus continued to love them and us all. He laid down His life for His bride, the Church, enduring suffering out of obedience to the Father and love for us.

Here is the model for husbands: "Husbands, love your wives, just as Christ also loved the church and gave Himself up for her." (Ephesians 5:25)

Marriage can be one of the most complicated relationships to love consistently, but that is by God's design. He uses the tension, the imperfections, and the struggles to purify both husband and wife. Through confession, forgiveness, repentance, and obedience, sin is purged, and the marriage begins to reflect God's image more clearly.

Sometimes this process requires suffering.

Furthermore, loving your wife when she opposes you means exercising self-control, resisting anger, and refusing to retaliate. James reminds us:

> "Let every person be quick to hear, slow to speak, slow to anger;
> for the anger of man does not produce the righteousness of
> God." (James 1:19-20)

When your wife seems like the enemy, don't let your flesh rise in attack. Instead, endure, love, and trust God with the outcome. After all, Jesus loved us even when we were unlovable.

But remember. Although retaliation may feel satisfying in the moment, it only creates disunity – like the tragic *War of the Roses* story we began with. Combat within marriage leaves spiritual casualties. Disunity in marriage distorts the reflection of God's image, like a cracked mirror that no longer gives an accurate picture.

So what can you do when your wife feels like the enemy?

- **Love your neighbor and remember, your closest neighbor is your wife.**

- **Love your wife by doing good to her.**

- **Love your wife by being a blessing to her.**

- **Love your wife by praying for her and yourself.**

Jesus summarized it this way:

> "You have heard that it was said, 'You shall love your neighbor
> and hate your enemy.' But I say to you, love your enemies and

pray for those who persecute you, so that you may be sons of your Father who is in heaven; for He causes His sun to rise on the evil and the good, and sends rain on the righteous and the unrighteous." (Matthew 5:43-45)

Love may demand sacrifice, patience, and endurance – but it is the way of Christ, and it is the way to restoration.

Love, in its truest form, is both tender and demanding. It requires sacrifice, but it also brings joy. As one anonymous writer put it:

"Love is a sweet tyrant, for the lover endures its torments willingly."

Marriage is not without its trials, but love – God's love flowing through you – makes the endurance worthwhile.

Conclusion

Marriage is a sacred covenant designed to reflect God's image, yet even within this holy bond, there will be seasons of conflict, hurt, and misunderstanding. At times, your wife may feel like your adversary. But God's Word calls you to rise above bitterness, retaliation, and withdrawal. Instead, you are commanded to love – with kindness, blessing, prayer, and steadfast commitment.

Christ loved His enemies, and He loved us when we were unlovable. As husbands, we are called to do the same for our wives. Loving your wife with the kind of love that is truly loving is not easy, but it is possible through the power of the Holy Spirit. Love does not ignore the pain, but it transforms how we respond to it. By choosing to love your wife even when she seems like the enemy, you are choosing the way of Christ – a way that leads to healing, reconciliation, and the reflection of God's glory in your marriage.

In the next chapter, we will discuss, "Loving your wife when she opposes your decisions."

Important Note

This chapter does not condone physical abuse of any kind. Please seek biblical counseling, pastoral guidance, and professional help. Your safety and the safety of your spouse matter to God.

Reflection Questions

1. When conflict arises, is my first response toward my wife marked by love, or by bitterness and defensiveness?

2. In what practical ways can I show kindness to my wife this week, especially if our relationship feels strained?

3. How can I bless my wife with my words and actions, even when I feel hurt by her?

4. What specifically do I need to pray for? Make a list. Then, schedule a time to begin regularly praying for your wife – not only for her needs, but also for your relationship and your own growth as her husband?

Chapter 7

Loving Your Wife When She Opposes Your Decisions

I once saw a commercial about a man with a severe plumbing issue. A pipe burst in his living room, flooding the house until the water was waist-deep. Panicked, he called a plumber. When the plumber arrived, toolbox in hand, he surveyed the mess and said, "This is serious. I'll get it fixed in no time."

But instead of letting him work, the homeowner smiled and replied, "Oh no... I only want an estimate." The plumber stood frozen, staring with disbelief as if to say, "You've got to be kidding me!"

Whenever I think of that commercial, it reminds me of my wife. Cynthia is a firm believer in getting estimates for repairs. I've lost count of how many times I've given her the same incredulous look that the plumber in the commercial above gave his customer. Many of our disagreements over the years have revolved around this issue. For me, if something breaks, I call a maintenance specialist, get an estimate, and – if it sounds reasonable – approve the job on the spot. Problem solved. But for Cynthia, one estimate is never enough. She believes it's unwise to move forward without comparing options.

This simple difference has sparked countless moments where I think, "You've got to be kidding me" in our marriage. But underneath the surface, these conflicts reveal something deeper. Like many husbands, the deeper issue is the tension that arises when our wives strongly oppose our decisions.

Decision-making in marriage is rarely straightforward. Our choices about home repairs, finances, health, or family priorities don't always align with our wives' perspectives. One reason for this is that most men, by nature, are task-oriented. We are workers who strive to complete tasks. Most wives are relational-oriented. They value relationships. Often, when our wives disagree with our husbands' decisions, it is not because they disrespect our leadership, but rather that we, as husbands, fail to value and consider their input. Too easily, we dismiss our wives as "too emotional" or impractical. But when we are quick to reject their ideas, they feel unheard, undervalued, and disrespected. This breeds frustration, which can turn even minor discussions into heated arguments. Before long, we may feel like we are never on the same page as our wives.

So, what can you do when decision-making becomes a point of conflict? Is there hope for unity in these moments? The answer is yes – but it starts with an honest question for us. When it comes to decision-making and your wife's ideas, the question you must ask yourself is: *Do I genuinely appreciate, affirm, and value my wife's contributions when decisions need to be made?*

Why Husbands Resist Their Wives' Input

If we're honest, many of us struggle to embrace our wives' input fully. Why?

- **We want to appear competent.** We fear that if we lean on our wife's perspective, she'll think we can't handle things on our own.

- **We fear comparison.** Deep down, some of us don't want our wives to think they're more intelligent or more capable than we are.

- **We fear failure.** Admitting she was right feels like admitting weakness. And if we make a poor decision after ignoring her advice, we dread the *"I told you so."*

- **We confuse leadership with control.** Some husbands believe that accepting their wife's influence diminishes their authority as head of the home.

- **We let pride get in the way.** We think more highly of ourselves then we should. Or we view ourselves as more logical than our wives.

- **We want to avoid conflict.** At times, we even hide problems from our wives to "protect them from worry," when in reality we are protecting ourselves from their emotional reaction.

But here's the truth: honoring your wife's input does not strip you of leadership. It does not diminish your God-given role as head of the home. Scripture makes it clear that God designed a divine order in both the Godhead and in marriage:

"The head of every man is Christ, the head of a woman is man, and the head of Christ is God." (1 Corinthians 11:3)

God still holds the husband accountable for the direction of the home, just as He called Adam to account after the fall in Eden. But accountability doesn't mean isolation. God gave Adam a helper suitable for him (Gen. 2:18-24), and He provides every husband with the same gift. Your wife is God's gift. Her role is not to compete with you, but to complement you. Ignoring her perspective is not a strength — it's folly.

So why should you respect your wife's input in decision-making? Scripture gives us at least three compelling reasons.

The Dangers of Rejecting Wise Counsel

Daniel and Sarah

Daniel had been married to Sarah for five years. He loved her deeply, but he often brushed aside her words when making decisions. "I know what's best," he would tell himself. "She worries too much."

One day, Daniel was offered a risky investment by a friend. Excited by the promise of quick profit, he rushed home to tell Sarah.

She listened carefully, then said, "Daniel, this sounds uncertain. Let's take time, pray about it, and seek advice before moving forward."

But Daniel waved off her concern. "I'm the head of this house. I know what I'm doing."

Without further thought, he poured their savings into the deal. Weeks later, the scheme collapsed, leaving them not only broke but struggling to pay their bills. The weight of his decision pressed heavily on him.

One evening, sitting at the kitchen table with his head in his hands, Daniel looked at Sarah. "I was wrong. I thought my way was right, but I ignored your wisdom."

Sarah reached for his hand. "We are partners, Daniel. God gave us to each other so we could walk wisely together."

If you made the same mistake as Daniel, would your wife respond to you like Sarah did with Daniel? Probably not. We'll save that discuss for another time.

But the point is that Daniel learned that night what Proverbs 12:15 had warned all along. What is the warning of Proverbs 12:15? Let's take a look.

The book of Proverbs draws a sharp contrast between foolishness and wisdom in decision-making. Proverbs 12:15 says,

"The way of a fool is right in his own eyes, But a wise man is he who listens to counsel."

This verse portrays a strong contrast between two types of people and how they receive advice from others.

The **fool** insists his way is always right. He refuses to listen to others, even when their advice is sound. Proverbs describes this person as gullible, arrogant, or stubborn – someone who repeats the same mistakes because he never learns from them. His pride blinds him, and his refusal to listen isolates him.

The **wise man**, on the other hand, humbly values counsel. He doesn't assume he has all the answers. Instead, he seeks perspective, considers input, and makes decisions that reflect discernment.

I once counseled a couple whose marriage was in crisis. After four sessions of counseling them separately, instructing them on the biblical role of a husband and wife, I brought them together to counsel them as a couple.

I asked his wife, "In light of your biblical role as a wife, how have you failed as a wife?" The wife humbly admitted her failures.

She said, "I have not always respected and submitted to my husband. And I often placed the children before him." With tears in her eyes, she committed to repent.

Then I asked the husband in what ways he had failed to love his wife as Christ loved the church.

To my surprise, he flatly replied, "I don't believe I've failed in any way."

After a long pause, he added, "Well, maybe in one way, I failed by not teaching her how to submit."

That statement revealed a heart unwilling to listen. I already spent four weeks with him, privately, instructing him regarding his biblical role as a husband. Yet, like the fool of Proverbs, he was convinced his way was right in his own eyes. Instead of humbly acknowledging his shortcomings, he deflected his responsibility. Scripture warns us that such pride leads only to frustration and failure (Prov. 14:1; Prov. 18:1–2).

As husband, we must ask ourselves: *Am I more like the fool who refuses to listen, or the wise man who welcomes counsel?*

If we are more like the wise man, Praise the Lord. But if we find that we are more like the foolish man, we must ask ourselves: If I am more like the foolish man who refuses to listen to wise counsel, then what changes do I need to make, going forward, to be wise and listen to the counsel of my wife?

The Blessings of Listening to Counsel

Proverbs 12:15 continues with, "But a wise man is he who listens to counsel."

A wise man is not simply intelligent; he is humble, teachable, and discerning. James describes it this way. He asks, "Who among you is wise and understanding? Let him show by his good behavior his deeds in the gentleness of wisdom." (James 3:13)

Wisdom shows itself not in arrogance but in humility – in the willingness to hear others, to weigh their words, and to act gently in response.

In considering your wife's opinion in decision-making, I am not suggesting that a husband should be passive and relinquish all responsibility of making decisions to his wife. A husband who loves his wife must value his wife's opinion. Your wife is your helper. She knows you better than anyone. She sees blind spots you may miss. Her counsel may not always be perfectly packaged (emotions can sometimes construe the message), but wisdom looks beyond delivery to discern the truth in what is being said.

Apart from the way your wife communicates her ideas, there is something else to consider. Sometimes, wives equate "listening" with "agreeing." If you don't follow their advice, they may feel unheard. As husbands, we must reassure our wives that listening does not always mean automatic agreement, but it does mean genuine consideration. The problem arises when we habitually dismiss their words. Over time, that pattern convinces them we never listen.

Listening means putting aside pride and giving serious thought to what she says. It doesn't require you to surrender leadership, but it does require you to demonstrate love by showing that her voice matters.

Proverbs remind us that, "Faithful are the wounds of a friend, but deceitful are the kisses of an enemy." (Proverbs 27:6)

Your wife is not only your partner but also your closest friend and neighbor. Sometimes her counsel may sting, especially if it points out uncomfortable truths. But those wounds can be the very thing God uses to sharpen and strengthen you. A wise husband receives correction with humility, evaluates it carefully, and adjusts where needed.

When you affirm your wife's counsel – not just by hearing it, but by acting on it when it proves wise – you honor her, build trust, and strengthen your marriage. There is a blessing when you consider your wife's counsel. But there is also a blessing when you honor your wife's ideas and opinions.

The Blessings of Honoring Your Wife's Input

Proverbs 15:22 reminds us that, "Without consultation, plans are frustrated, but with many counselors they succeed."

Likewise, Proverbs 24:3-6 declares:

> "By wisdom a house is built, and by understanding it is established; And by knowledge the rooms are filled with all precious and pleasant riches. A wise man is strong, and a man of knowledge increases power. For by wise guidance, you will wage war, and in abundance of counselors there is victory."

The principle is simple: wise counsel leads to blessing. And one of the most significant sources of wise counsel in your life is your wife.

I've seen this firsthand. As I shared earlier, my wife Cynthia is a firm believer in getting multiple estimates before major repairs. For years, I resisted her advice, thinking my way was quicker and more efficient. But when I finally listened and sought more than one estimate, I was amazed at how much money we saved. Her wisdom made us better stewards of what God entrusted to us.

I've also learned valuable lessons from her about shopping. Early in our marriage, I would rack up debt at department stores, convinced I was getting good deals. When Cynthia challenged me, I bristled – taking her correction as an attack on my competence rather than as wise counsel. But when I finally humbled myself and tried her approach, the results spoke for themselves. Instead of spending more and coming home with less, I managed to go home with more gifts for less money. And instead of conflict, her words turned into encouragement: *"Thank you for listening. Thank you for valuing my input."* That affirmation deepened our trust and drew us closer together.

Her counsel has even impacted my health. Like many men, I thought I was invincible. I ignored aches, pains, and even illnesses, dismissing her attempts to urge me to see a doctor. But over time, I realized she was right – I'm not invincible, and ignoring health concerns only hurts both of us. Listening to her has helped me to do a better job caring for my physical health, so I can continue to prolong my life and walk alongside my wife in our journey together.

The truth is, when we respect our wives' input, we strengthen not only ourselves but also our homes. We build marriages marked by unity, trust, and blessing. We exercise the spiritual disciples of a wise husband.

Conclusion

When it comes to making decisions, Scripture reminds us:

> "Do nothing from selfishness or empty conceit, but with humility of mind regard one another as more important than yourselves; do not merely look out for your own personal interests, but also for the interests of others." (Philippians 2:3-4)

Marriage is not about one spouse always getting their way. God designed husbands and wives to complement, support one another, and work together as a unit. While the husband bears the ultimate responsibility as the head of the home, he dishonors his role when he ignores the wise counsel that God has given him through his wife.

Valuing your wife's input does not mean surrendering leadership. It means leading with humility, wisdom, and love. When your wife sees that her thoughts matter – even if you don't always follow her advice – she feels respected, honored, and cherished. And that builds trust and unity in your marriage.

In the end, we learn from both our right and wrong decisions. But when we humble ourselves enough to listen to our wives, we often discover blessings, avoid unnecessary mistakes, and grow closer as one.

As the anonymous saying goes:

"No one learns to make the right decisions without being free to make wrong ones."

The difference is whether we allow pride to isolate us – or wisdom to guide us into partnership.

In the next chapter, we will discuss, "Loving your wife when you feel unappreciated."

Reflection Questions

1. When my wife offers input, do I truly listen with humility, or do I quickly dismiss her ideas?

2. In what areas of life (finances, health, household, parenting) could I benefit from valuing her counsel more?

3. How can I communicate to my wife that I respect her thoughts, even when I choose a different course of action?

4. What practical steps can I take this week to invite my wife into decision-making, rather than making choices in isolation?

Chapter 8

Loving Your Wife When You Feel Unappreciated

Robert and Sharon

Robert and Sharon had been married for six years and were raising two young children – a two-year-old son and a four-year-old daughter. Robert works as a maintenance supervisor at a local hospital, while Sharon works from home as a business consultant, earning twice Robert's income. They came to counseling as a last attempt to save their marriage.

Sharon expressed her frustration, stating, "Robert doesn't contribute enough to our marriage. I work all day while also managing the kids, the finances, and household responsibilities. Everything falls on my shoulders. He takes no initiative and leaves most of the decisions to me. Whenever I ask for help, his response is, *Whatever you decide is fine with me.*"

Robert, visibly angry, countered: "Nothing I do is ever good enough. Just last week, I repaired the garage door, redid the landscaping, and spent an entire day with the kids so she could have a break. I cook dinner at least four nights a week. But she doesn't acknowledge any of it. Instead, she always focuses on what I didn't do right. No matter what I do, she never appreciates it. And here's what I've realized – it's my fault. I've spent our whole marriage trying to win her approval, make her happy, and avoid conflict."

Sharon laughed bitterly: "Making me happy? Well, it's not working – I'm not happy!"

Robert snapped back, "Fine. Maybe I should move out."

The Problem

- Sharon has unmet expectations.

- Robert craves appreciation and approval.

- Sharon has assumed leadership in the home.

- Robert has become passive.

- Sharon has a dominant personality.

- Robert mistakenly believes his role is to make Sharon happy.

The Result — A reversal of roles, escalating chaos, and deep frustration.

A Desire to Be Appreciated

Every husband longs to be appreciated. I know I do. But what does appreciation really mean, and what does it look like in practice?

Appreciation is simply recognition and gratitude. It means acknowledging someone's contributions, holding them in high regard, and expressing thankfulness for who they are and what they do. To appreciate someone is to value them — not just for their actions, but for their presence, character, and efforts. When you are grateful for someone, you acknowledge, recognize, cherish, and value who they are and what they contribute.

So, how can a wife show appreciation to her husband? Here are some simple yet powerful ways:

- Saying "thank you" often and sincerely

- Writing a short note or card of gratitude

- Sharing what she admires about him in front of others

- Verbally recognizing his strengths and contributions

- Valuing his opinions and ideas

- Offering gentle correction without belittling

- Respecting his decisions without a bad attitude, even when she dis agrees

- Rewarding his efforts with special gestures (a favorite meal, a back rub, or planned time together)

Why does appreciation matter so much? Because when a wife acknowledges and values her husband, it strengthens him. Appreciation motivates him to keep giving, encourages him to do more, and builds his confidence. It feeds his sense of significance, reminding him that his efforts make a difference.

When your wife makes you feel valued, it motivates you to do better. When your wife shows gratitude, it makes you feel good about what you have done and are doing. It makes you feel good about yourself. It feeds your ego, that is, your self-esteem, and makes you feel significant. And when both a husband and wife reciprocate appreciation, it strengthens their relationship. It is a tremendous blessing to the soul to know that someone values, admires, and recognizes your importance. Sure, it is easy for your wife to point out what you could do better. All of us are a work in progress. We are far from perfect. Nonetheless, most husbands want to know that their wives appreciate them. And so do wives. But here's the question: *When does a healthy desire for appreciation become sinful?*

How Far Are You Willing to Go to Receive Appreciation?

Wanting your wife's appreciation is normal. But is pleasing her your primary goal as a husband? Or is your goal something greater?

Robert, in our opening story, believed the breakdown of his marriage came from his constant pursuit of Sharon's approval. He spent years trying to keep her happy, but no matter what he did, it was never enough. The truth is, no husband can fully satisfy his wife's expectations 100 percent of the time. To make her constant happiness your mission is an impossible burden.

So what motivates a husband to devote himself to such an unachievable pursuit? The answer lies in the heart's motives.

When the Desire for Approval Becomes an Idol

Scripture warns us against allowing good desires to become ultimate ones.

- Isaiah wrote, "But the rest of it he makes into a god, his graven image. He falls down before it and worships; he also prays to it and says, 'Deliver me, for you are my god." (Isaiah 44:17)

- James stated, "But each one is tempted when he is carried away and enticed by his own lust." (James 1:14)

What is an idol? An idol is anything – visible or hidden – that takes the place of God in our hearts. An idol is what we look to for comfort, security, or identity. And often, idols are not carved statues but desires of the heart.

For many husbands, the desire for appreciation can quietly become an idol. Approval becomes the "god" they bow to, the thing they must have to feel significant. And where you have idolatry, you also have lust. Lust is what fuels idolatry – not only longing for the object itself, but for the gratification it provides. What is lust? Lust is something a person longs for as a means of self-gratification and fulfillment. Lust is the feeling of pleasure that a person desires and must have. An Idol is the object of worship, but lust is the pleasure or personal benefit that one craves and seeks to enjoy that the object provides. In other words, a person can worship an object, but that object is merely a means to an end, satisfying one's desires. In essence, what compels a person to worship an idol is the enjoyment of what the idol provides.

What do idolatry and lust have to do with a husband's desire for appreciation? A husband may crave appreciation, affirmation, validation, or peace at any cost.

The desire to be respected, affirmed, or valued is not sinful in and of itself. Most husbands long for these things. But when these desires turn into demands, they reveal idolatrous lust. The heart begins to say, *"I must have her approval to feel whole."*

And when a husband builds his life around his wife's approval, he not only makes her an idol – he falls into another trap: **the fear of man.**

The Fear of Man

Proverbs 29:25 warns: "The fear of man brings a snare, but he who trusts in the Lord will be exalted."

Although we have discussed the "fear of man" more extensively in chapter 4 of this book, it is worth mentioning again as it relates to a husband whose ambition is to seek his wife's approval. When a husband becomes overly concerned with his wife's approval, he falls into this snare. His worth becomes tied to her opinions. He may avoid making decisions to keep the peace, stay silent when he should speak truth, or hide how he really feels for fear of rejection. His leadership erodes, not because his wife demands it, but because he has surrendered his leadership role in exchange for affirmation.

This is the danger of living for appreciation: it turns leadership into passivity, courage into silence, and love into wife-pleasing.

Unbiblical Responses to Feeling Unappreciated

When some husbands feel undervalued, it's tempting to respond in ways that only worsen the problem. Here are some common but unbiblical responses of husbands who feel unappreciated by their wives:

- **Passivity:** Relinquishing leadership and letting your wife take over, hoping it will reduce conflict.

- **Bitterness and Anger:** Harboring resentment instead of addressing issues in love (Eph. 4:26, 31).

- **Retaliation:** Withholding affection, neglecting responsibilities, or intentionally frustrating her as a form of punishment (Rom. 12:17).

- **Avoidance:** Intentionally working late, withdrawing emotionally, or shutting down communication to escape conflict (Eph. 4:25).

- **Manipulation:** Threatening to leave or making dramatic statements you don't mean, using fear to gain control. Example: *Maybe I married the wrong person.*

None of these responses honors God. They may feel natural in the moment, but they only deepen disunity and dishonor the covenant of marriage.

So, the question remains: *"If these are the wrong responses, how should I respond when I feel unappreciated?*

How Should You Respond When You Feel Unappreciated?

When you feel unappreciated, Scripture calls you to look to Christ. Husbands are commanded to love their wives as Christ loved the church – and Christ's example shows us how to respond when gratitude is lacking.

Consider the story of the ten lepers:

"While He was on the way to Jerusalem, He was passing between Samaria and Galilee. As He entered a village, ten leprous men who stood at a distance met Him; and they raised their voices, saying, 'Jesus, Master, have mercy on us!' When He saw them, He said to them, 'Go and show yourselves to the priests.' And as they were going, they were cleansed. Now one of them, when he saw that he had been healed, turned back, glorifying God with a loud voice, and he fell on his face at Jesus' feet, giving thanks to Him. And he was a Samaritan. Then Jesus answered and said, 'Were there not ten cleansed? But the nine—where are they? Was no one found who returned to give glory to God, except this foreigner?' And He said to him, 'Stand up and go; your faith has made you well.'" (Luke 17:11–19)

Jesus healed ten lepers, but only one-a Samaritan outsider–returned to give thanks. Jesus noticed the ingratitude of the nine, yet He did not retract His gift of healing. He let them enjoy the blessing even though the majority of them failed to appreciate Him as the giver.

What does this mean for husbands? Simply this: at times, your wife may fail to show gratitude. Others – friends, co-workers, even strangers – may express more appreciation for you than your wife. But like Jesus, you are called to continue doing good, even when thanks is absent.

Jesus taught this principle plainly when he said:

"But love your enemies, and do good, and lend, expecting nothing in return; and your reward will be great, and you will be sons of the Most High; for He Himself is kind to ungrateful and evil men. Be merciful, just as your Father is merciful." (Luke 6:35–36)

When your wife doesn't seem to appreciate you, respond with mercy, compassion, patience, and kindness. Mercy reflects Christ's character. As Henry Ward Beecher once said:

No one thing does human life more need than a kind consideration of the faults of others. Everyone sins; everyone needs forbearance. Our own imperfections should teach us to be merciful.

Mercy means continuing to do good without demanding a return. It means refusing to give up, even when gratitude is lacking. The Apostle Paul re-emphasizes this principle when he said,

> "Let us not lose heart in doing good, for in due time we will reap if we do not grow weary. So then, while we have opportunity, let us do good to all people, and especially to those who are of the household of the faith." (Galatians 6:9–10)

So, don't let discouragement harden you. Keep loving, keep serving, and keep doing good – not because your wife always appreciates it, but because God sees, God rewards, and God is glorified.

Show Appreciation for Your Wife

One of the best ways to encourage appreciation in your marriage is to model it yourself. Paul gives this counsel in his letter to the Philippians when he wrote,

> "Finally, brethren, whatever is true, whatever is honorable, whatever is right, whatever is pure, whatever is lovely, whatever is of good repute, if there is any excellence and if anything worthy of praise, dwell on these things. The things you have learned and received and heard and seen in me, practice these things, and the God of peace will be with you." (Philippians 4:8–9)

Paul reminds us to focus our thoughts on what is praiseworthy. Applied to marriage, this means intentionally dwelling on the good in your wife rather than the shortcomings.

- **What is true?** She loves you, even if imperfectly. She has stood by you in your failures. That loyalty is worth celebrating.

- **What is honorable?** Maybe she faithfully provides for the children, or shows care for your needs. Honor her sacrifices.

- **What is right?** At times, you know she is correct in what she says – acknowledge it instead of minimizing it.

- **What is pure?** Does she strive to live a life pleasing to the Lord? Does she care for your home with integrity? Recognize her pursuit of purity.

- **What is lovely?** Notice the small ways she shows she cares – in her appearance, beauty, her touch, or thoughtfulness.

- **What is of good repute?** Reflect on her talents, gifts, and strengths that benefit your family.

Don't just dwell on these things silently – express them verbally. Tell your wife directly what you admire about her. Share words of praise privately and publicly. When a husband openly affirms his wife, especially in front of others, she feels valued and honored.

And here's the blessing: Paul promises that when we practice this discipline of dwelling on what is praiseworthy, *the God of peace will be with you* (Phil. 4:9). Peace flows into marriages where gratitude is both practiced and spoken.

Even better, when you consistently model appreciation, it may inspire your wife to reflect that same gratitude and appreciation to you.

Share Your Heart with Your Wife

If you feel wounded because your wife doesn't seem to appreciate you, the answer isn't silence or anger – it's honest, loving communication.

The Apostle Paul modeled this kind of transparency with the church in Corinth. Paul told the church,

> "We have spoken freely to you, Corinthians, and opened wide our hearts to you. We are not withholding our affection from you, but you are withholding yours from us. As a fair exchange—I speak as to my children—open wide your hearts also." (2 Corinthians 6:11–13, NIV)

Paul, Timothy, and the others who worked with Paul showed love and affection for the Church in Corinth, but it was not reciprocated. Yet, Paul didn't lash out in frustration; instead, he opened his heart, appealed with affection, and invited reciprocity.

Husbands are called to do the same. If you feel unappreciated, speak the truth in love. Share your feelings honestly, not with accusations or attacks, but with vulnerability, sincerity, and care.

James gives us a practical safeguard for being too quick to respond to people without giving careful thought to the situation before speaking.

James wrote, "Everyone must be quick to hear, slow to speak and slow to anger; for the anger of man does not achieve the righteousness of God." (James 1:19-20)

All of us have received emails or text messages from someone, and we misconstrue what they said, responded too quickly, without thinking, and end up having to apologize and ask for forgiveness for our response. Share your heart with your wife. But act, don't react. Think about what you are going to say, being mindful that knee-jerk reactions are not always the best.

Moreover, as you share your heart with your wife, be careful not to "talk at" your wife with phrases like, *"You never. You always. You don't..."* These words land like daggers and close her heart. Instead, "talk to" her with words that reveal your feelings. For example, start the conversation with the following statements:

- "Here's how I feel when this happens..."

- "I feel discouraged when it seems my efforts go unnoticed..."

- "It hurts when I don't feel valued, because I deeply love you and want to serve you."

Speaking this way communicates your heart without attacking hers. It opens the door for understanding and reconciliation. However, keep in mind that sharing your heart with your wife in this way does not always guarantee that she will respond well to what you share. If she does not respond well, then you may need to put your words to paper. Write her a love letter.

More than anything. If your wife makes even small efforts to change, acknowledge them! Be her encourager. Be her cheerleader. Affirm her growth. If you fail to recognize her efforts, even small ones, she may quickly lose motivation. Just as husbands need appreciation, so do wives. Encouragement is fuel for both hearts.

Face Reality

Appreciation is a beautiful gift, but your wife will not always show it – no matter how hard you try or how well you serve. Expecting constant recognition is setting yourself up for disappointment.

Your wife's approval is not your purpose as a husband. While it is good to desire gratitude, it should never be your ultimate motive for loving her. Your calling is higher: to love her as Christ loves the church, whether she notices or not.

Seek to Please the Lord

What is your purpose in life? What is your goal as a husband? Paul reminds us of our ultimate aim: "Therefore we also have as our ambition, whether at home or absent, to be pleasing to Him." (2 Corinthians 5:9)

Colossians 3:17 emphasizes this principle when it says, "Whatever you do in word or deed, do all in the name of the Lord Jesus, giving thanks through Him to God the Father."

Your goal as a husband is not to secure appreciation from your wife but to glorify God. Love your wife faithfully, sacrificially, and unconditionally because it pleases the Father. Jesus laid down His life for the church, not because the church deserved it, but because it honored His Father and fulfilled His mission (Eph. 5:25-28).

In the same way, your love for your wife is an act of obedience and worship. Whether she affirms you or not, your commitment to love her reflects Christ and brings glory to God.

When you commit to living the life of Christ, you can overcome the challenges of loving your wife.

Conclusion

The desire to be appreciated is not wrong — it's deeply human. But when that desire becomes an idol or a demand, it enslaves you. True freedom comes when you shift your focus from seeking your wife's approval to seeking God's pleasure.

Your wife may not always notice your sacrifices. She may not always say "thank you." But God sees. God rewards. And God calls you to continue doing good, even when appreciation is absent.

Love your wife — not because she always applauds you, but because Christ loved you when you were unworthy. In doing so, you will not only honor your marriage but also glorify the Lord who has called you to this sacred role.

Reflection Questions

1. When I serve my wife, am I motivated more by her approval or by a desire to please the Lord?

2. In what ways has the desire for appreciation become an idol in my life?

3. How can I model appreciation for my wife this week, both privately and publicly?

4. What would it look like for me to keep loving and serving my wife faithfully, even when I don't feel appreciated?

Conclusion
Overcoming Challenges to Loving Your Wife

Marriage is a sacred calling, one that requires patience, humility, and a steadfast commitment to live out the love of Christ. Each chapter of this book has revealed not only the real struggles that husbands face but also the unshakable truth that God has given us the strength, wisdom, and grace to love our wives faithfully through it all. Living the life of Christ gives us the victory.

In Chapter 1, we began by asking the question, "Where is the love?" That search leads us not to fleeting emotions but to the everlasting love of Christ, which becomes the foundation for our marriages. True love is not merely a feeling; it is a choice, a commitment, and a reflection of God's covenant with us. This is why it was necessary to define love clearly (Chapter 2), grounding it in Scripture as patient, kind, and sacrificial—never self-seeking or conditional.

But what happens when the road is hard? When it feels as though your wife does not love you back (Chapter 3) or refuses to respect your authority (Chapter 4)? Here, the call of Christ becomes even more urgent: to love without expecting return, to serve without demanding recognition, and to lead with humility, just as Christ loved the church, even when we were unworthy.

Moreover, living the life of Christ, will help overcome offenses. When offenses cut deep (Chapter 5), we are reminded that forgiveness is the hallmark of divine love. To hold grudges is to choke the life out of marriage; to forgive is to let God's mercy flow through us. And even when our wives may feel like our enemies (Chapter 6), we are commanded to bless, not curse; to pray, not resent; to fight for oneness, not against one another.

Furthermore, leadership in marriage also means standing firm when your decisions are opposed (Chapter 7). Loving your wife by living the life of Christ, in these moments, requires courage balanced with tenderness, conviction wrapped in compassion. Finally, when your sacrifices to love your wife go unseen or unappreciated, Chapter 8 reminds your that your service is first unto the Lord. God sees every act of faithfulness, even when it is overlooked by human eyes.

Taken together, these lessons point to one unshakable truth: loving your wife is not always easy, but it is always holy. Every challenge becomes an opportunity to mirror Christ's relentless love. Every disappointment becomes a chance to lean on God's strength rather than your own. Every sacrifice becomes a living testimony of the gospel in action.

As you close this book, may you be reminded that your marriage is not just about companionship—it is a ministry. It is your daily chance to live out the life of Christ before the one He has entrusted to you. Choose to love, even when it is hard. Choose to forgive, even when it hurts. Choose to persevere, even when you feel unseen. In doing so, your marriage will not only endure but shine as a witness to the transforming power of God's love.

Let your home become a living example of the gospel. And may your wife see in you, day by day, a reflection of Christ Himself.

Final Charge

Husband, your greatest calling is to love your wife as Christ loves His church. Do not wait for her actions to determine your devotion; let your love flow from the cross, where Christ first loved us. Rise each day with a renewed commitment to serve, to forgive, and to lead with humility. When you love her this way, you honor God, strengthen your marriage, and reflect the very heart of Christ to the world.

Our Closing Prayer

Heavenly Father,

We thank You for the gift of marriage and for the sacred calling You have placed on husbands to love their wives as Christ loves the church. Lord, we confess that this calling is greater than our strength, but we rest in the promise that Your grace is sufficient.

Teach us to love patiently and kindly, without envy, pride, or anger. Teach us to forgive as You have forgiven us. Strengthen us to lead our homes with humility, to serve with joy, and to lay down our lives daily as Christ laid down His for us.

When challenges come, remind us that love never fails. When we feel unseen, remind us that You see and reward every act of faithfulness. And when our love feels weak, fill us again with Your Spirit, so that our marriages may shine as a living testimony of the gospel.

We commit our marriages into Your hands. May our homes be filled with peace, unity, and the presence of Christ. And may our love be a reflection of Your unending love for us.

In the mighty name of Jesus, Amen.

About the Author

Dr. Darrell Rose serves as Associate Pastor and Director of Maturity at Good Hope Missionary Baptist Church in Houston, Texas. He holds a Bachelor of Arts in Biblical Counseling from the College of Biblical Studies in Houston, a Master of Arts in Biblical Counseling from The Master's University and Seminary in California, and a Doctor of Ministry with a concentration in Biblical Counseling from Southern Baptist Theological Seminary in Louisville, Kentucky.

A certified biblical counselor and Fellow member of the Association of Certified Biblical Counselors (ACBC). Dr. Rose is recognized for his deep commitment to equipping others in gospel-centered care. In 2024, he taught a session on "Counseling Those Who Grieve After Suicide" at the ACBC Annual Conference in Fort Worth, Texas, reflecting his dedication to addressing life's most painful challenges with biblical clarity and compassion. Rose has taught church leaders on, "Counseling Techniques for Restoring Broken Marriages," at the 2025 Power Walk and Baptist Fellowship Association Leadership Conference at the Noah's Ark Museum in Williamsburg, Kentucky.

Dr. Rose is the author of What Every Husband Needs to Love His Wife: The Essentials and Rewards, and co-author, alongside his wife, Cynthia Rose, of Marriage Without Misery: Moving from Chaos to Conformity in Christ. Together, they have shared their insights at numerous marriage retreats, pastoral leadership conferences, and counseling workshops across the country.

Dr. Rose and Cynthia are proud parents of two adult sons and joyful grandparents of three. To learn more, visit or contact him at drose@goodhope.org.

Notes

1. Guy Njoukam, "Inspire Others: 100 Inspirational Stories that would Change Your Life." Middletown, DE 2017

2. C. E. Copen, Daniels K. Vespa, J. Mosher, First marriages in the United States: Data from the 2006–2010 National Survey of Family Growth. National health statistics reports; no 49. Hyattsville, MD: National Center for Health Statistics. 2012

3. http://healthresearchfunding.org/55-surprising-divorce-statistics-second-marriages/

4. William E. Vine, Vine's Expository Dictionary of Old Testament and New Testament Words (Nashville, TN: Thomas Nelson, 1940), 547.

5. Lawrence Richards, "Richards Complete Bible Dictionary," (Iowa Falls, IA. World Bible Publishers. 1984), 473.

6. John MacArthur, (Ed.). (1997). https://ref.ly/logosres/macartsb?ref=Bible.Col3.12&off=1290&ctx=late d %E2%80%9Cgentleness%2c%E2%80%9D+~it+is+the+willingnes (electronic ed., p. 1838). Nashville, TN: Word Pub.

7. David Powlison and J. Yenchko, Article: "Should We Get Married? Five 'Pre-Engagement Questions to Ask Yourself,'" The Journal of Biblical Counseling. Vol. 14, Number 3., Spring 1996

8. Zick Rubin, Ph. D., www.verywell.com

9. R. H. Rottschafer, Benner, David G. and Peter C. Hill. B. Baker Encyclopedia of Psychology & Counseling 2nd Ed. Baker Reference Library. Grand Rapids, MI: Baker Books, 1999

10. L. Leyden, "On Being Human: Why Are We Here?" http://www.magic al-living.com (accessed July 5, 2010).L. Leyden, "On Being Human."

11. https://en.wikipedia.org/wiki/Counterfeit

12. www.HappyWivesClub.com

OVERCOMING THE CHALLENGES OF LOVING YOUR WIFE
Living the Love of Christ

STUDY GUIDE

STUDY GUIDE

Addressing the Obstacles that May Hinder Husbands from Loving Their Wives

Chapter 1: *Where is the Love?*

Session Theme: Rediscovering biblical love in marriage and understanding why passion fades, conflicts rise, and disunity often takes root.

Summary

This chapter begins with a sobering story of a husband ready to leave his wife—only to rediscover love too late. It asks a piercing question: *Where is the love?*

- Love in marriage often fades after the excitement of dating and early years.

- Husbands and wives drift apart through selfishness, disrespect, and unresolved conflicts.

- Divorce is not ultimately caused by lack of passion, but lack of biblical love.

- Paul's call in **Colossians 3:12–15** shows that the glue of marriage is agape love—compassion, kindness, humility, gentleness, patience, forgiveness, and above all, love.

- Love is not emotion-driven but Spirit-enabled. God equips husbands to choose love daily.

Key Scriptures
- **Colossians 3:12–15**, "Beyond all these things put on love, which is the perfect bond of unity."

- **Ephesians 5:25** – Husbands are commanded to love as Christ loves the Church.

- **Philippians 2:12–13**, God works in us to will and act according to His good pleasure.

Group Discussion Questions
1. How does your current love for your wife compare to the love you showed when dating or newly married?

2. Which "garments" from Colossians 3 (compassion, kindness, humility, gentleness, patience, forgiveness) are weakest in your marriage right now?

3. What are some signs in your marriage that point to selfishness rather than sacrificial love?

4. Why is "lack of love" a more accurate biblical explanation for divorce than "loss of passion?"

5. How does relying on the Holy Spirit change your ability to love your wife daily?

Practical Application
- **Daily Check-in:** Each morning, ask yourself: *What is one way can I "put on love" toward my wife today?* Write it down and do it.

- **Intentional Communication:** Plan one uninterrupted 20-minute conversation with your wife this week where you only listen—no phone, no TV, no multitasking.

- **Date Night Reset:** Recreate one intentional gesture from your dating years (flowers, a note, a meal, or a walk).

- **Conflict Pause:** When tension rises, pause and silently pray Colossians 3:12–14 before responding.

- **Accountability Partner:** Share with another husband in the group the specific "garment" you're working on this week. Check in midweek to encourage each other.

Love in Action (Weekly Challenge)
- Personal Step: Identify one specific "garment" (Colossians 3:12–14) you need to put on. Practice it intentionally with your wife this week (e.g., patience in conflict, kindness through service, forgiveness for a past hurt).

- Prayer Commitment: Each day this week, pray: *"Lord, help me put on Your love toward my wife today."*

Leader's Notes (Optional)
- Begin with the story at the start of the chapter—it will draw men in emotionally.

- Encourage honest reflection without shaming. Many will resonate with "the drift" described.

- Keep the group focused on solutions: Spirit-empowered love, not just human willpower.

- Reinforce confidentiality; some men may confess difficult feelings about their marriage.

Chapter 2: *Love Defined*

Session Theme: Understanding the biblical definition of love—moving from cultural feelings to Christlike choices.

Summary

Many men equate love with provision—working, protecting, providing. While important, these fall short of the **Christlike love** commanded in Scripture.

- The world defines love as passion, feelings, or attraction.

- The Bible defines love as **agape**: unconditional, sacrificial, action-oriented.

- Ephesians 5:25 calls husbands to love as Christ loved the Church by giving Himself up.

- 1 Corinthians 13 describes what love *is* (patient, kind) and what it *is not* (envious, boastful, self-seeking).

- Love is not sustained by emotions but by the Spirit of God. True biblical love is a daily decision rooted in obedience, not convenience.

Key Scriptures

- **1 Corinthians 13:4-7**, Love's definition in action.

- **Ephesians 5:25** – Husbands, love your wives sacrificially.

- **Romans 12:9-10**, Love must be sincere, honoring others above ourselves.

Group Discussion Questions

1. How has your understanding of love been shaped by culture, family,

or past experiences?

2. Which attribute of love in 1 Corinthians 13 (patience, kindness, humility, perseverance) is most challenging for you?

3. In what ways do you find yourself confusing "provision" for "love?"

4. What is the difference between feeling love and choosing love?

5. How does Christ's sacrificial example challenge the way you approach your marriage?

Practical Application

- **Love Inventory:** List the traits of love from 1 Corinthians 13. Circle the ones you struggle with most. Share one with the group and commit to working on improving in your area of weakness this week.

- **Replace Feelings with Actions:** Instead of waiting to "feel" love, choose one action daily to demonstrate love to your wife (helping with chores, listening, affirming words, or initiating prayer).

- **Practice Sacrifice:** Do something this week that costs you comfort, time, or convenience, purely to bless your wife.

- **Scripture Meditation:** Read 1 Corinthians 13:4–7 aloud each day. Insert your own name in place of "love" (e.g., "John is patient, John is kind...") to personalize the text.

Love in Action (Weekly Challenge)

Write your wife a letter or note identifying one way you are choosing to love her intentionally this week—regardless of circumstances or emotions. Follow through on it.

Leader's Notes (Optional)

- Stress the distinction between cultural love (emotion-based) and biblical love (Spirit-enabled choice).

- Encourage men to admit where their love has been transactional or conditional.

- Push the group toward action: love is proven in practice, not theory.

- Allow men to share their "love inventories" in a safe, supportive way.

Chapter 3: *Loving Your Wife When Love Is Not Returned*

Session Theme: Choosing Christlike love even when your wife does not return it reflects Jesus' love that perseveres despite rejection.

Summary

- Christ loved us while we were still sinners, before we responded to Him (Romans 5:8).

- In marriage, husbands will sometimes feel their love is ignored, unreciprocated, or dismissed.

- Biblical love (*agape*) is not dependent on being appreciated or returned—it is a deliberate act of the will.

- Loving without return is not weakness; it is obedience to Christ and an opportunity to demonstrate His unconditional love.

- God rewards faithfulness to His command, even when earthly responses are lacking.

Key Scriptures

- **Romans 5:8** – Christ loved us while we were still sinners.

- **Matthew 5:44-46**, Love your enemies and those who do not love you back.

- **1 Peter 2:23** – Jesus entrusted Himself to the Father when mistreated.

Group Discussion Questions

1. When have you experienced giving love without receiving it in return (in marriage or other relationships)?

2. How do you typically respond when your love feels unreciprocat-

ed—withdrawal, anger, apathy, or persistence?

3. Why does Romans 5:8 challenge our natural instincts in marriage?

4. What are some unhealthy expectations you sometimes place on your wife's responses?

5. How can trusting God's reward help you love unconditionally when your wife doesn't respond?

Practical Application

- **Shift Your Focus:** Instead of asking *"How is she responding?"* ask *"Am I obeying Christ in love?"* Journal daily on this perspective.

- **Silent Service:** Do one act of love this week without pointing it out or expecting thanks (e.g., clean something, prepare something, handle a task quietly).

- **Pray for Her:** Pray specifically for your wife's needs each day, asking God to bless her, without praying for her to change toward you.

- **Gratitude Reset:** Write down three qualities you appreciate about your wife, even if she isn't showing love back in the moment.

Love in Action Challenge

Choose one tangible way to serve your wife this week **without telling her** and without expecting acknowledgment. Offer it as worship to God.

Leader's Notes (Optional)

- Prepare men for emotional honesty—this session may stir feelings of loneliness, rejection, or disappointment.

- Stress that God measures love by obedience, not reciprocity.

- Remind men that love without return mirrors Christ's love for us.

- Encourage testimonies at the next meeting of how God worked in them as they loved unconditionally.

Chapter 4: Loving Your Wife When It Seems She Does Not Respect Your Authority

Session Theme: Exercising biblical authority through servant leadership, not domination, passivity, or demanding respect.

Summary

- Many husbands confuse authority with control, while others retreat into passivity or adopt egalitarian confusion.

- Domination damages wives and children, leaving wounds of disrespect, fear, and disunity.

- Passivity poisons marriages, creating distance, resentment, and disorder.

- Egalitarianism, while affirming equality, often erases God-given roles and produces division.

- True biblical headship reflects Christ: servant leadership, humility, sacrifice, and love (Eph. 5:23; Mark 10:42–43).

- Husbands are called not to demand respect but to love their wives as Christ loved the Church—even when respect feels absent.

Key Scriptures

- **Mark 10:42-43**, Greatness is found in servanthood.

- **Ephesians 5:23, 28-29**, Husbands as servant-leaders, nourishing and cherishing their wives.

- **1 Corinthians 11:3** – God's divine order in marriage.

- **Romans 5:8** – Christ loved us despite our lack of respect for His authority.

Group Discussion Questions

1. Which tendency do you see more in yourself—domination, passivity, or retreat into "peace-faking?" How has it affected your marriage?

2. How does Jesus' model of servant leadership challenge the way you exercise authority at home?

3. Why is demanding respect counterproductive in marriage?

4. In what ways does loving your wife sacrificially—even when she doesn't respect you—reflect Christ's love for you?

5. What would it look like in your home if your leadership was marked more by service than by control?

Practical Application

- **Servant Leadership Exercise:** Choose one task this week that your wife normally carries alone (e.g., dishes, bedtime with kids, scheduling) and take it on as an act of service.

- **Encouragement Plan:** Speak one intentional word of encouragement to your wife each day this week.

- **Self-Check:** Journal when you feel tempted to demand respect. Ask: *Am I leading with humility or seeking control?*

- **Christlike Model:** Re-read Mark 10:42-43 daily. Write one way you will apply it in your leadership at home.

Love in Action Challenge

This week, intentionally serve your wife in one area where she least expects it, without mentioning "authority" or "respect." Let your actions reflect Christ's leadership.

Leader's Notes (Optional)

- Emphasize that biblical authority is God-given, not earned by income, strength, or demands.

- Help men identify whether they lean more toward domination or passivity.

- Stress that servant leadership is not weakness—it reflects the strength of Christ.

- Invite men to share practical stories of serving their wives in humility at the next session.

Chapter 5: *Loving Your Wife When She Has Offended You*

Session Theme: Forgiving as Christ forgave—breaking the cycle of resentment and choosing restoration over retaliation.

Summary

- Offenses are inevitable in marriage—harsh words, unmet expectations, careless actions.

- Unforgiveness builds walls of bitterness, resentment, and distance.

- Forgiveness is not forgetting or excusing—it is releasing the right to revenge.

- Paul calls husbands to "bear with one another and forgive one another... just as the Lord forgave you" (Col. 3:13).

- Choosing forgiveness mirrors Christ, who forgave us at the greatest cost.

- A forgiving husband creates an environment of grace where intimacy can thrive.

Key Scriptures

- **Colossians 3:13** – Forgive as the Lord forgave you.

- **Matthew 18:21-22,** Forgive not seven times, but seventy times seven.

- **Ephesians 4:31-32,** Be kind and tenderhearted, forgiving one another.

Group Discussion Questions

1. What is one offense from your marriage that was hardest for you to forgive? How did it impact your relationship?

2. Why is it easier to hold onto grudges than to forgive?

3. How does Christ's forgiveness of you shape your ability to forgive your wife?

4. What happens to intimacy in a marriage when unforgiveness is left unchecked?

5. How do you distinguish between true forgiveness and just "sweeping things under the rug"?

Practical Application

- **Forgiveness Journal:** Write down one offense you're still holding against your wife. Pray over it daily this week, asking God for the strength to release it.

- **Replacement Practice:** Each time a memory of the offense resurfaces, replace it by speaking a word of blessing over your wife.

- **Prayer of Release:** Verbally pray, "Lord, I release this offense and choose to love my wife as You have loved me."

- **Bridge-Building Action:** Do something kind for your wife in the very area where offense has taken root (e.g., if she hurt you with words, write her an encouraging note).

Love in Action Challenge

Identify one specific offense you've been carrying and **release it to God this week.** If appropriate, tell your wife, "I forgive you," and follow it up with a loving action.

Leader's Notes (Optional)

- Some men may open up about deep hurts—protect confidentiality.

- Clarify that forgiveness does not excuse sin but reflects obedience to Christ.

- Remind participants that forgiveness is often a process—sometimes daily.

- Encourage testimonies of small steps of forgiveness to inspire others.

Chapter 6: *Loving Your Wife When Life Feels Like an Enemy*

Session Theme: Loving your wife when she feels like your adversary by choosing Christlike love, kindness, blessing, and prayer over bitterness and retaliation.

Summary

- Marriage can experience seasons where love turns into conflict, and your spouse may even feel like an enemy.

- Yet, Scripture calls husbands to love their wives unconditionally, reflecting Christ's love for the Church.

- Loving in times of tension requires supernatural grace expressed through kindness, blessing, prayer, and steadfast endurance.

- By following Christ's example, husbands can move from division to restoration and reflect God's image more clearly in their marriages.

Key Scriptures

- Matthew 22:37-39, The command to love God and your neighbor.

- Luke 10:27 – Love God fully, love your neighbor as yourself.

- Luke 6:27-28 – "Love your enemies, do good to those who hate you, bless those who curse you, pray for those who mistreat you."

- Ephesians 5:25 – "Husbands, love your wives, just as Christ also loved the church and gave Himself up for her."

- James 1:19-20, Be quick to hear, slow to speak, slow to anger.

Group Discussion Questions

1. What emotions or reactions typically surface when your wife feels like

your opponent?

2. Why do you think bitterness is such a powerful enemy of love in marriage?

3. How does Jesus' teaching about loving your enemies reshape the way husbands should respond in conflict?

4. What are some practical acts of kindness you can show your wife when your relationship feels strained?

5. In what ways can blessing and prayer soften both your heart and hers during conflict?

6. How does Christ's example of loving the Church encourage and challenge husbands?

Practical Application
- Choose one act of kindness this week to surprise your wife, even if tension exists.

- Speak one word of blessing to your wife daily — highlighting something you admire or appreciate.

- Pray specifically for your wife's needs, your own growth, and your relationship together.

- When tempted to retaliate, pause and practice James 1:19 — listen, slow down, and pray.

Love in Action Challenge
Each day this week:
1. **Do good** – one tangible act of kindness.

2. **Bless** – one intentional word of encouragement or affirmation.

3. **Pray** – intercede for your wife and your marriage.

Write down what changes you notice — in her, in yourself, and in the atmosphere of your home.

Leader's Notes (Optional)

- Remind the group: This teaching does not condone abuse. We can offer help for the perpetrator, but the safety of the victim always comes first.

- Encourage vulnerability but maintain respect — avoid spouse-bashing or unhelpful criticism

- Guide men back to Christ as the model: loving sacrificially, enduring patiently, forgiving continually.

- Emphasize that love is an act of the will, not just an emotion — and it requires dependence on the Holy Spirit.

- Suggest accountability partners within the group to check in on the weekly challenge.

Chapter 7: *Loving Your Wife When She Opposes Your Decisions*

Session Theme: Leading with humility and dependence on God when disagreements arise.

Summary

- Disagreements in marriage are inevitable, but they can create division when husbands react with pride or defensiveness.

- Many husbands equate leadership with "winning the argument," but biblical leadership looks like humility, prayer, and seeking God's will.

- Proverbs 3:5–6 reminds us to trust in the Lord, not our own understanding, and He will direct our paths.

- Christlike leadership listens carefully, values input, and ultimately seeks God's wisdom above ego.

- When opposed, the husband's role is not to dominate, withdraw, or avoid—but to shepherd his home with patience and prayer.

Key Scriptures

- **Proverbs 3:5-6**, Trust the Lord in all decisions.

- **Proverbs 15:22** – Without consultation, plans are frustrated, but with many counselors they succeed.

- **Proverbs 18:2** – A fool takes no pleasure in understanding, but only in expressing his opinion.

- **James 1:5** – Ask God for wisdom, and He will give generously.

Group Discussion Questions

1. How do you typically react when your wife disagrees with your decision—anger, withdrawal, defensiveness, or prayer?

2. What does Christlike leadership look like in the face of opposition?

3. How can involving your wife in prayer before decisions strengthen your marriage?

4. What's the difference between leading with humility versus leading with pride?

5. How do you discern whether a disagreement is about preference or about principle?

Practical Application

- **Prayer Before Action:** Commit to pray with your wife before making one significant decision this week.

- **Listening First:** In your next disagreement, allow her to fully share her perspective before offering yours.

- **Decision Journal:** Write down a decision you're facing. Record how you sought God's wisdom and how your wife's input shaped your thinking.

- **Check Your Motive:** Before making a final call, ask: "Am I choosing this for her good and God's glory, or to protect my pride?"

Love in Action Challenge

Before making one significant decision this week, pray with your wife and seek God's direction together.

Leader's Notes (Optional)

- Emphasize that leadership is stewardship, not control.

- Encourage men to be humble—remind them that asking for input is not weakness but wisdom.

- If pride or defensiveness arises in discussion, point men back to Christ's servant-leadership as the model.

- Allow time for sharing personal stories of decisions made well (or poorly) and lessons learned.

Chapter 8: *Loving Your Wife When You Feel Unappreciated*

Session Theme: Serving faithfully even when unnoticed, remembering that God always sees.

Summary

- Every husband longs to be appreciated, but often love and sacrifice go unnoticed at home.

- Feeling unappreciated can lead to resentment, withdrawal, or anger if left unchecked.

- Jesus Himself often went unrecognized and unappreciated, yet He continued to serve in love.

- Matthew 6:4 reminds us that God sees what is done in secret and will reward openly.

- A Christlike husband chooses to love and serve not for applause, but for obedience to God.

Key Scriptures

- **Matthew 6:4** – Your Father who sees in secret will reward you.

- **Galatians 6:9** – Do not grow weary in doing good, for in due season you will reap.

- **Colossians 3:23-24**, Work heartily, as unto the Lord, not for men.

Group Discussion Questions

1. When was the last time you felt unappreciated in your marriage? How did you respond?

2. Why do you think appreciation is so important to us as husbands?

3. How does focusing on God's reward rather than your wife's recognition change your perspective?

4. What dangers arise when unappreciation turns into bitterness?

5. How can you create habits of serving in secret, like Jesus?

Practical Application

- **Secret Service:** Do one intentional act of service for your wife this week without telling her or seeking acknowledgment.

- **Gratitude Shift:** Keep a short daily gratitude list of 3 ways your wife contributes to your life, even if she doesn't thank you in return.

- **Reward Reminder:** Memorize Colossians 3:23–24 and repeat it when tempted to feel unnoticed.

- **Reframe Resentment:** When you feel unappreciated, ask: *Am I serving for her thanks or for God's glory?*

Love in Action Challenge

This week, perform a thoughtful act of love for your wife **in secret**—allowing God alone to see it as your worship.

Leader's Notes (Optional)

- Encourage honesty—many men struggle deeply with lack of appreciation.

- Remind participants that Christ is the model: He gave everything while many rejected Him.

- Reinforce that God always sees, and His reward is greater than human recognition.

- Celebrate testimonies of men who served in secret and how it impacted their mindset.

Conclusion: *The Fruit of Christlike Love*

Session Theme: Overcoming the challenges, in your marriage, by living the love of Christ as a lifelong calling that transforms you, your wife, your family, and your legacy.

Summary

- Loving your wife as Christ loves the Church is not a one-time effort—it is a lifelong pursuit.

- The fruit of Christlike love is transformation: in your character, your marriage, your family, and even future generations.

- John 13:34–35 reminds us that love is the distinguishing mark of Christ's disciples.

- When husbands consistently love sacrificially, their marriages become testimonies of the gospel.

- True success in marriage is not measured by comfort or recognition, but by faithfulness to God's calling.

Key Scriptures

- **John 13:34-35,** Love one another as I have loved you.

- **Galatians 5:22-23,** The fruit of the Spirit includes love, patience, and kindness.

- **1 John 4:19** – We love because He first loved us.

Group Discussion Questions

1. Looking back, what is one way you've grown in Christlike love through this study?

2. Which habits or practices (prayer, forgiveness, service, sacrifice) do you want to carry forward after this group ends?

3. How has your perspective on leadership and love in marriage shifted?

4. What do you hope your children, friends, or community will learn by watching your marriage?

5. How will you continue seeking accountability to remain faithful in loving your wife as Christ loves the Church?

Practical Application

- **Personal Reflection:** Write down the top three lessons God has taught you during this study.

- **Covenant of Love:** Create a written commitment or prayer with your wife, declaring your desire to love her like Christ loves the Church.

- **Accountability Partner:** Pair with another man from the group to check in monthly on your marriage journey.

- **Family Legacy Action:** Share with your children (if applicable) one lesson you've learned about love and model it at home.

Love in Action Challenge

Share with your wife what you've learned in this study, and identify one specific way you will continue to grow in Christlike love moving forward.

Leader's Notes (Optional)

- This is a capstone session—encourage celebration of progress and testimonies of growth.

- Invite participants to share their biggest takeaways from the study.

- Consider ending with a group covenant of accountability or prayer of dedication for all marriages represented.

- Encourage ongoing fellowship beyond the study (small groups, mentoring, prayer partners).